SCANIA

SCANIA

TRUCKS TODAY

Eric Gibbins

MOTOR RACING PUBLICATIONS LTD
28 Devonshire Road, Chiswick, London W4 2HD, England

ISBN 0 900549 58 0
First published 1980

Photosetting by Zee Creative Ltd., London SW16.
Printed in Great Britain by The Garden City Press Limited,
Letchworth, Hertfordshire SG6 1JS.

Contents

About the author

ERIC GIBBINS is one of Britain's most experienced and highly respected commercial-vehicle writers with a journalistic career dating from 1953, when he joined *Motor Transport* as an editorial assistant. He subsequently became assistant editor of that journal before taking over the editorship of the magazine *Commercial Vehicles* in 1962. He left journalism for a short period in order to take up a senior public relations appointment within the industry, but by 1970 he was once again writing full-time, soon to become editor and publisher of the *Freight Industry Yearbook* and *Truck & Bus Builder*. His intimate knowledge of all aspects of the commercial-vehicle industry, and in particular of truck design, construction and operation, has been invaluable in ensuring the accuracy and authority of these one-make histories in the TRUCKS TODAY series.

Introduction

In writing this book about Scania — the first in the series *Trucks Today* — I have endeavoured to include as much about the way in which the company has developed worldwide as about the Scania products.

The first chapter deals with the history of Scania until 1960. It is essentially a scene-setter for the rest of the book, which explores the paths taken by Scania in vehicle design, manufacture, research and development and marketing, which have made the company a force to be reckoned with not only in its native Sweden, but also throughout Europe and in other selected areas of the world.

As a member of the transport press, it has been fascinating for me to compare Scania as it was when I first visited it in the early-1960s with the company today. The only thing that has not changed is the helpfulness of its personnel, and here a special word of thanks must go to Sven Nylin and Bo Bjorkman for their untiring efforts on my behalf in digging out facts, figures and photographs.

Eric Gibbins

The first ever demountable bodies? In 1909 Scania introduced this design with a passenger-carrying body which could be dismounted and replaced with a flat load-carrier.

Chapter 1

Prelude to the boom years

Twenty years ago, if the road transport pundits of the day had been asked which commercial vehicle manufacturers would be among the European leaders in 1980, it's unlikely that more than a handful would have mentioned the name Scania, or Scania Vabis as it was then. Yet today, in terms of really heavy commercial vehicle production — that is, 16 tons gross weight and over — Scania ranks as number three in Europe with a 1979 global production figure of 22,140 vehicles in that weight class out of a total production of some 25,000. It is also a real force internationally in commercial vehicle manufacture, with modern plants not only in Sweden, but in The Netherlands, Brazil and The Argentine.

This book sets out to explain how this has come about, concentrating on this 20-year period during which it has all happened. The only European companies which bettered the 1979 Scania performance on a worldwide basis in this 16 tons-plus market category are the market leader, Daimler-Benz, with 52,048 vehicles, and Iveco (Magirus Deutz and Fiat) with 29,950.

Compare this with the scene 40 years earlier (in 1939 to be precise) when the total annual production at Scania was 300 vehicles. In the postwar era, manufacturing figures were still calculated in hundreds rather than thousands, despite a boost to the company's activities caused by the Swedish Government's World War 2 demand for military vehicles for defence, even though Sweden, of course, was never involved with the hostilities.

Outside Sweden in the postwar years, it was still very much a case of 'Scania-who?', even though the company had been around for some time. Its origins, like so many of the vehicle manufacturing pioneers, go back to the 1890s — to November 5, 1891, in fact — when the board of directors of an iron founders called Surahammars Bruk formed the VABIS company. It was just as well they called it VABIS, because if they had used the full name the company would have been doomed from the start. Imagine the foreigner trying to get his tongue around the full name of the company from which VABIS stems — Vagnfabriksaktielolaget i Södertälje — which stands for Wagon Factory Company in Södertälje. The original object of forming this company was to build railway goods wagons.

Those first directors must have been shrewd, not only for choosing a short, easily identifiable and marketable name, but for recognizing early on the rosy future for road vehicle production. Within six years, VABIS had built its first road vehicle, a tiller-steered private car.

From that point the company never looked back; it was wedded to road vehicles. The Scania part of Scania-VABIS was added in 1911 when Scania, which had built its first four-wheeled road vehicle — also a car — in 1901, joined forces with VABIS. Scania was based at Mälmo but, although production continued there up to the mid-1920s, Södertälje became the headquarters of the joint company.

Although car production was carried on for two decades,

Scania's first car was a Vabis, built in 1897 and seen here on test. It is now in the Museum of Technology, in Stockholm.

production if they seemed right. Many manufacturers, especially in the past, have fallen into the trap of designing their goods vehicles in isolation, as an engineering exercise, without looking at them as the means of solving a particular transport problem. Whether that was true of Scania in the pre-World War 2 period is difficult to say, but certainly it has not been so in the past two decades. Scania seems to have been very aware that basically they are making tools to do a particular job — to move goods from one place to another — and that those tools must be made to do those jobs in the most efficient way possible.

In so doing they have satisfied the needs of the vehicle operator. However, they have paid equal attention to another important person — the driver — and this, as will be seen, has been a main factor contributing to the company's expansion and success.

Neither characteristic, however, was particularly apparent in the hand-building days up to 1939. In fact, it was not until

there was an increasing emphasis on commercial vehicles for, as early as 1902, both Scania and VABIS had launched their first goods vehicles.

People often say that there is nothing new in automotive design, and this is certainly true of an idea which Scania used on its very first commercial vehicle models, which today is regarded as one of the most advanced forms of distribution system. This is the demountable body. Scania produced its first example in those early days of the 1900s; there was a passenger-carrying body which could be lifted off and replaced with a goods vehicle body.

It was not until 1924 that Scania abandoned its private car building interests and, incidentally, closed down the Malmö operation, centering commercial vehicle production at Södertälje. This coincided with a development which, once again, revealed a characteristic, continually to be found in this Swedish company, of never being shy about experimenting with new designs and putting them into

The first Vabis truck — a 1½-tonner — was built in 1902 and entered commercial service the following year.

Scania has always had an eye for producing vehicles to suit particular work. In 1923 the company introduced this hydraulic-action three-way tipper, which had a considerable impact on highway construction work.

well after the end of World War 2 that the first signs were evident. There were, of course, one or two notable developments between the world wars and it is worth picking out a few highlights.

Following experimental applications, propeller-shaft drive, for example, was introduced as standard in 1924 and it was in the same year that Scania introduced its first three-axled vehicle with a tandem-drive bogie and fitted pneumatic tyres. However, three-axled vehicles did not really catch on in Scandinavia until the 1930s. Scania also produced a double-reduction axle design and this, together with a progressive semi-elliptic spring design developed in this period, aroused considerable interest amongst bus operators because of the improved vehicle ride characteristics it gave.

As the 1920s closed, Scania brought out its 'bulldog' bus design, a forward-control unit with the driver's seat alongside the engine. A truck version of the same chassis came along in 1935, but as indicated later, forward-control was not to be favoured for many years to come.

It was in this period of the late-1920s and early-1930s that Scania first moved towards diesel engine use. The first power units of this type were produced to a design developed by Jonas Hesselman. These Hesselman engines were started on petrol and then, when warmed up, switched to diesel. This was a 65 horsepower engine and it was used up until the late-1930s, after Scania had produced its own proper diesel engine in 1936. This power unit took the company through to the end of World War 2, although a new range of engines, to be known after 1949 as the D-series, had first made its appearance in 1939. These were modular in-line **engines**

Scania's head office and main factory is located in this lakeside setting at Södertälje, just south of Stockholm.

were still responsible for a very high proportion of this total. The export explosion was starting, but its real force had yet to come. The signs were there, however. Scania started local assembly of vehicles on the outskirts of Sao Paulo, Brazil, in 1953 and established a full-scale factory there in 1956.

At the same time, Scania was laying the foundations of the design concepts which were to bring success to the company in the future. Had the management then been wrong about any one of its several basic design paths there is little doubt that Scania today would be no force at all in the marketplace.

Probably the most critical area in this respect was in engine development. Scania — who, as already indicated, built its first diesel, a pre-combustion chamber type producing 120 bhp, in 1936 — pinned its faith to turbocharged diesel engines as far back as 1951. That year it announced an in-line eight-cylinder direct-injection diesel developing 180 bhp as a naturally aspirated engine and 205 bhp in turbocharged form. The importance of this lay in the fact that it was considered to

available in four, six and eight-cylinder form. In the war years, whilst Sweden was starved of oil, it had plenty of timber and large numbers of vehicles were converted to operate on wood burning producer gas units. These were to disappear just as soon as oil supplies were resumed in 1945.

Although Sweden was not involved in the 1939-45 conflict, the Swedish Government nevertheless put its armed forces on a war footing, which meant large orders for Scania for tanks, cross-country vehicles, army lorries and troop transporters. Manufacturing facilities were expanded and production streamlined so that, when peace came in 1945, the company was well-equipped to satisfy the demand for vehicles in a transport-starved Europe. Not that Scania sold many vehicles outside its traditional markets — the Scandinavian territories. In fact, sales outside Scandinavia could virtually be counted on the fingers of one hand, or maybe two.

This situation was not to change until the 1950s, following the setting-up in 1949 of an export department; 300 vehicles were sold abroad in 1950. In 1955, some 1,600 trucks and buses were exported, but the other Scandinavian countries

Bonneted models were favoured strongly in Scandinavia up to the 1960s, when there was a noticeable move to forward-control designs, although this rig, from the 1960s, was typical of the outfits run at that time by the Swedish haulage co-operatives. Note the use of the lifting trailing axle on the hauling vehicle — a feature in widespread use in Sweden for light-laden running.

Direct-acting air brakes were introduced by Scania in 1954 and hydraulic power steering the following year on a range of bonneted L-series vehicles such as this impressive-looking bulk carrier. These innovations were way ahead of their time.

Weight and length limits in Sweden, as reflected by the outfit above, gave Swedish manufacturers a tremendous advantage in the 1960s in that they had long experience of producing the types of vehicle which were suddenly in demand. The container revolution had created a need for vehicles to carry containers of up to 30 tons weight, but in Sweden it was permitted to carry two 20ft-long boxes of up to 40 tons on a big artic. Thus vehicles had to be scaled-down to meet other countries' requirements. Here is a semi-trailer with a Hulo trailing axle.

be the world's first turbocharged diesel engine to go into series production. A Swiss-made Brown Boveri turbocharger was used. This happened at a time when many diesel engine design engineers considered turbocharging of diesels to be a basically incorrect concept as a standard practice because it resulted, they considered, in high wear and failure rates.

Scania's success, however, is underlined by the fact that it established the principle of designing engines specifically for turbocharging. The first Scania diesel built with this in view was developed in the 1950s, turbocharger design work in Europe and the USA being carefully monitored, and it was launched as the DS10 in 1961. In naturally aspirated form, as the D10, this engine developed 165 bhp, but a modest 24 per cent turbocharging factor caused it to produce 205 bhp. Today, a majority of Swedish (not just Scania) diesel engines are turbocharged.

As Scania has pointed out, by adopting turbocharging and by designing engines specifically for turbocharging, high outputs and better fuel consumption figures can be achieved. Technical development has led to durability and reliability characteristics being appreciably improved over the years.

For Scania, the 1950s laid a firm foundation for success in the next two decades. I recall visiting Sweden for the first time and remember noticing how very few forward-control vehicles were operating there then. Virtually all the big timber-hauling tractor units, coupled up to as many as three or four trailers, were bonneted models. No babies, these rigs, they could be almost any length up to 80ft long and weigh as much as 52 tons.

As in most countries, however, there had been a steady build-up to this weight level, legislation changing with road improvements and being linked directly to axle weight limits. Up to 1950 in Sweden the highest permitted axle load varied between 3 and 6 tons, and it was not until 1951 that 6 tons was generally permitted on main highways. On rural roads it was 5 tons or less.

Axle and bogie load limits went up steadily in the 1950s until, by 1962, axle load limits of 8 to 12 tons were permitted on 67 per cent of Sweden's road network, with lower weights on other roads. Then, in the 1960s, the formula was changed to permit 10/16 ton axle loads, and vehicles to meet these

Progress in timber-hauling by Scania. Above, a purpose-built road train dating from before World War One and, above right, a typical L71 design, fitted with Scania's 150 bhp diesel engine and built in 1955, on heavy-duty forestry work.

A measure of the tough operating conditions which generated Swedish vehicles can be detected in this 1951 picture showing a load of timber being toppled on skids from an LS60 truck.

The first Scania diesel of 1936 developed 120 bhp and had indirect injection using heater plugs to aid starting.

limits steadily increased in numbers as the roads on which they could operate also steadily increased. Today, 10/16 tons is permitted on over 90 per cent of the Swedish road network.

Nowadays, this axle weight legislation — which has other more detailed rules — effectively permits the operation of vehicles of up to 51.4 tons. Vehicle length was not controlled until 1967 when a limit of 24 metres (78ft 9in) was introduced.

Even as late as 1967, it was recorded in *Commercial Vehicles International* that the majority of Scania-Vabis trucks (the name had become Vabis instead of VABIS by then) had a normal-control layout. Strangely, perhaps, it was in the upper end of the gross weight ranges that forward-control models were replacing their bonneted counterparts

for on-highway operation. The length of time that Scania stayed with bonneted models is perhaps a little surprising as the company was one of the first in Europe to build forward-control vehicles. Nevertheless, bonneted models dominated demand. This remained so right up to the 1970s. In 1975, on a worldwide production basis, 55 per cent of all Scanias delivered were still bonneted models, although by 1979 the figure had become 40 per cent bonneted to 60 per cent forward-control. This did not reflect the situation in the European market, of course, where 90 per cent of all vehicles sold were forward-control.

Understandably, vehicles have to be strong and powerful to cope with the rigours of Swedish use, like timber-hauling at the weight mentioned, especially when surfaces are rough, gradients are steep in mountainous regions, and there are roads on which snow and ice may lie for several months of the year. Against this operational background it is not difficult really to pinpoint the reasons for Scania's success in the 1960s and 1970s. The base created in the 1950s was as solid as a rock, with designs which were powerful, strong and built for reliable operation at high weights.

In the 1960s, when the era of the big European truck dawned — for motorway use, international haulage and freight container carrying — Scania was ready. Low weight and restrictive dimension laws in many countries, notably Britain, where the workhorse was the 24 tons gross eight-wheeler, meant that the vehicle-manufacturing industries of those countries were used only to producing what today would be regarded as medium-weight vehicles. Scania virtually started where they left off and, as soon as the weight limits were raised, they had a complete range of vehicles available — off the peg as it were — with all the componentry necessary for operation at up to 52 tons, which by then was the Swedish weight limit. It was then a question of marketing them.

Innovation in the 1920s. A Scania Post Bus adapted for snowy conditions and hauling a sledge trailer.

This Scania dating from the late-1950s was the lightest vehicle in a range which at that time went up to the LS71, a 6 × 4 tractive unit.

17

This L51, being used on milk collection, was one of the most popular models of the 1950s. It was fitted with the 100 bhp D442 engine and the G50 five-speed synchromesh gearbox and was built from 1953 to 1959.

Two options with trailer-hauling in 1948. Above right, an LS23 three-axled design from the L20 range hauling a single-axled trailer and carrying timber for wood pulp, and right, a two-axled L13 from the L10 range with twin-axled trailer attached hauling concrete blocks.

The trend towards forward-control
Showing the shift in Scania's production from bonneted to forward-control designs

	1960	1963	1970	1975	1979
Total number of vehicles delivered	5,210	9,390	12,590	17,300	22,250
Percentages of bonneted and forward-control vehicles delivered					
Bonneted	100	90	59	55	40
Forward-control	—	10	41	45	60
Bonneted					
7-8 litre engine	50	39	22	6	3
10-11 litre engine	50	51	37	46	35
14 litre engine	—	—	—	3	2
Forward-control					
8 litre engine	—	—	14	12	14
10-11 litre engine	—	10	23	25	24
14 litre engine	—	—	4	8	22

The best sellers in the 1940s — the L10

Scania's bonneted L10 series was built in its original form from October 1944 to November 1946. It was a two-axled design fitted with the 90 bhp D402 four-cylinder diesel engine and K40 four-speed crash gearbox. Built for operation at 7.5 tons gross weight, it was offered in wheelbases ranging from 3.4m to 4.6m. A new version of the L10 with modifications, including improved braking, appeared in November 1946 and continued in production until 1949; it included a 9-ton model.

Over 1,500 of the original and revised L10s were produced in this period. The revised version of the L10 was accompanied by the introduction of a more powerful model, the L20, also a two-axled machine, but with a 135 bhp engine and the K45 four-speed crash gearbox, a power train specification which was also found in the LS20, the three-axled version. The L20 four-wheelers, in wheelbase versions up to 5m, were intended for operation at 10 tons and 11 tons gross weight, while the designed gross weight of the LS20 six-wheeler was 15 tons.

Scania's first forward-control cab, which was produced in the early-1930s. Forward-control was not to displace bonneted units for many years.

The first L10s, like this example with cattle-carrying bodywork, appeared in 1944 and the series was to prove best-sellers for the next five years.

The shape of things to come. This L21, powered by the 135 bhp D604 engine, operated in 1948 between Stockholm and Paris with a payload of 15 tons.

How about this for a bonnet! This 1941 dump truck had its D801 engine converted to wood-burning producer-gas power.

The best sellers in the 1950s — the L40 and L51

Over 2,000 bonneted L40s were built by Scania between December 1949 and March 1953. This two-axled design originally matched the 90 bhp D422 diesel with the four-speed K40 crash gearbox, but later, from July 1951, the G50 five-speed synchromesh unit was adopted. A spread of wheelbases from 3.8m to 4.6m gave payloads of 9 tons and 9.5 tons according to specification.

The L60 was the more powerful version, basically built for operation at 10 tonnes, and was produced between 1949 and 1954 and fitted with the 135 bhp D622 diesel engine. This, too, started off with the four-speed crash box, then switched in 1951 to the five-speed synchromesh gearbox. The LS60 was the six-wheeled version with payloads up to 15.5 tons.

The L51 bonneted series replaced the L40s in April 1953 and was produced until June 1959. This was powered by the D442 four-cylinder diesel which, at 100 bhp, produced 10 bhp more than the D422. The five-speed synchromesh box was now a standard fitment. Close on 2,000 of these L51s were built. Designed for gross weights of 10 tons and 11 tons, the L51 models had wheelbases ranging from 3.8m to 5.03m.

There were also the more powerful versions, the two-axled L71s with the six-cylinder diesel producing 150 bhp, and the three-axled LS71s fitting the same engine. Both had the five-speed synchromesh gearbox and were built for operation at 16 tons gross weight.

An example of the LS60 series which, with its four-wheeled counterpart, the L60, was introduced in 1949 and manufactured until 1954.

Built in 1953, this L61 tractor unit is shown hauling a tank semi-trailer and a further semi-trailer with front-axle bogie to give a gross weight of 26.7 tons.

Shortage of diesel oil fuel led to the use during World War Two of wood-burning producer-gas vehicles like this Scania built in 1941.

Scania's B16 bus chassis built from 1945 to 1949 formed the basis of this dust cart. It was powered by the D402 engine producing 90 bhp.

Above right, an example of the LS60 range built from 1949 to 1954. This bulk cement-carrying vehicle has the 135 bhp diesel engine and G50 five-speed synchromesh gearbox. Right, one of the last L7138s, fitted with a Meiller dump truck body, which was built in 1957 just before the introduction of the L75 series.

Introduced in 1946, the L20 series was fitted with the D604 engine. This picture is of a 1948 L20 tractor unit pulling a Fruehauf tank semi-trailer with a capacity of 9,470 litres.

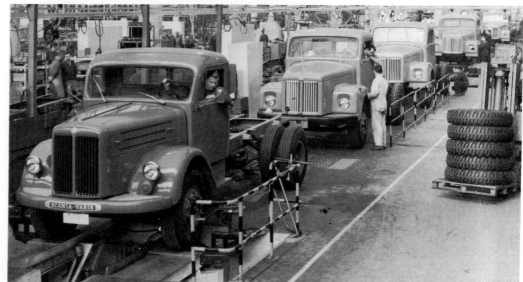

Final assembly and inspection of a group of L60-series vehicles which, together with the LS60 models, were in production from 1949 to 1954.

Chapter 2

Model development

Scania entered the 1960s as Scania-Vabis, but it began the 1970s as Scania, the decision having been made to drop the Vabis name in 1968. At the same time the company discontinued using its old bicycle-chain-wheel symbol. Then, in 1969, came the merger between SAAB and Scania.

Before taking a look at the development of the Scania product in the 1960s and 1970s it is appropriate to take a sideways glance at this link-up between these two Swedish giants, especially, perhaps, in view of the speculation at the time about one aspect — the Volkswagen marketing franchise for Sweden held by Scania (and which Scania still holds in 1980) through its subsidiary company Svenska Volkswagen.

It was in the immediate postwar years that Scania-Vabis started selling Volkswagens, and its success was such that by the mid-1960s it had sold some 450,000 VWs in Sweden and had more than 300 VW service and repair shops.

On the face of it, therefore, a merger between SAAB and Scania might have affected the Volkswagen activity, but this does not seem to have happened; the organization appears to be as strong as ever, selling 20,659 Volkswagens in Sweden in 1978 — just 7,000 less than SAAB itself in the same year.

The decision in favour of a proposed merger of SAAB and Scania-Vabis was made by the respective boards of directors in 1968. However, the actual amalgamation did not take place until May 1970, at a shareholders' general meeting. As with the VW franchise, the merger has had little direct impact on Scania's truck-building operations, the structure of the SAAB-Scania parent company fostering the independent development of Scania as an autonomous organization under the cover of its umbrella. This cover is formidable just for the back-up available to Scania, if and when required, for it embraces a wealth of technical know-how in many fields, not least in electronics and computers.

In 1980, the Scania Division of SAAB-Scania AB, to give both organizations their correct titles, is the largest division in SAAB-Scania and employs over 40,000 people.

Scania says that the basic tenet of its product philosophy — and it is one which has been applied for many years — is the concentration of product development on medium-heavy and heavy vehicles, the company indicating that a clear limitation is imposed on variants to achieve batch production of the most important vehicle models.

Scania's policy has always been not only to design its own truck from front to back, but to design and build all major components, so not only does the company build its own engines, but also its gearboxes, axles, frames and cabs.

This policy — in strict contrast with that of other manufacturers (particularly the American truck builders) who consider it right to use the best proprietory engines, gearboxes or axles available — has been a platform of Scania's production policies throughout the 1960s and 1970s.

As already indicated, at the beginning of the 1960s, normal-control, bonneted designs dominated the scene, and the L75 was the best seller.

The forward-control Scania LB76 running as a conventional articulated outfit and seen here with a fully refrigerated semi-trailer.

Two of the 1980 T-series trucks being evaluated at the Södertälje test track, where the facilities include steep hills, a water bath and all kinds of road surfaces.

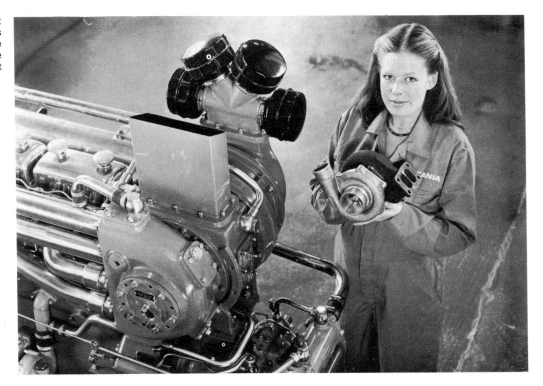

The turbocharger installed on the first turbocharged diesel engine to enter series production in the early-1950s — the Scania D815 (left) was about six times the size of the efficient and compact turbochargers in use in the late-1970s.

Both naturally-aspirated and turbocharged diesel engines of Scania's own design were offered throughout the range, the power levels of the trucks offering much higher than average power-to-weight ratios than comparable European vehicles of that period.

Gearboxes, also of Scania's own design remember, were synchromesh on all forward speeds. Synchromesh was an unusual feature on heavy trucks of this period. Yet another unusual feature was the fitment of power steering on most models — a reflection of higher weight limits and much tougher operating conditions in Scandinavia than in other parts of Europe. Fitment of power steering went hand-in-hand with better-than-normal suspension and ride characteristics.

Then there was the cab. Although this had some outdated features, these were more than compensated for by the high quality of the interior fittings and appointments, particularly in respect of heating, ventilation and insulation. It was above all robust, a feature which Scania was to exploit to the full when mounting sales drives in overseas markets. Sweden had its own strength test. It was — and still is — a legal requirement that a truck cab must be able to withstand an impact from a 1 ton weight falling in a pendulum from a height of 3 metres and hitting the cab from different directions. In addition, the cab roof is exposed to a static pressure of 15 tons. In both instances, the door must not open and the deformations that result must not be so great that they trap the driver or passengers.

An essentially-Swedish characteristic which distinguished Swedish (not just Scania) designs of the early-1960s was the use of heavy-duty, three-axle artic tractor units and load carriers with a single driving axle, the third undriven axle being fitted with a bogie lift to permit it to be raised when travelling unladen so as to reduce tyre wear and scrub — and the turning circle. It was also used to improve traction when required. With a slight lift of the trailing axle, axle weights can be altered on the front and driving axles.

The double-drive bogie was virtually non-existent, the Swedish argument being that fitment of an air-operated differential lock on a three-axled machine with a single driving axle meant that traction problems on muddy or uneven surfaces could be overcome, thereby making the double-drive bogie unnecessary. Overseas demand, however,

created a market for 6 × 4s with the result that today double-drive bogies are offered as an alternative to a 6 × 2 configuration on all three-axled models.

As for brakes, although two-circuit, direct-acting air brakes with a third system for the parking brake were fitted to a few vehicles at this time, Scania already knew they were the systems of the future; they were first offered by Scania in 1954 and became standard on Scania trucks and buses in 1962.

In terms of engines, the Scania range of the day centred on the fitment of the then new family of engines, the D-series. The first of these was the D10, which was a six-cylinder, 10.25 litre naturally-aspirated power unit developing 165 bhp at 2,200 rpm and a maximum torque of 456 lb ft at 1,200 rpm. Other D-series engine models followed, production being

Scania decided at a very early stage on a policy of building all its major components, and throughout the 1960s and 1970s moved towards a programme of rationalization which by 1980 had resulted in the standardization of three basic engines, three gearboxes and three back axles for the T-series models.

consolidated on the D8, D11 and D14 designs.

A manufacturer's design philosophy is not always easy to expound. However, with Scania it is possible to cheat a little because John Rönnhult, head of Scania's chassis development laboratory, conveniently produced a paper as Scania moved from the 1960s into the 1970s which set out the company's aims. His subject was safety aspects of commercial vehicles and, in dealing with this topic, he

The LB76 in artic tractor form, this being a 1964 example.

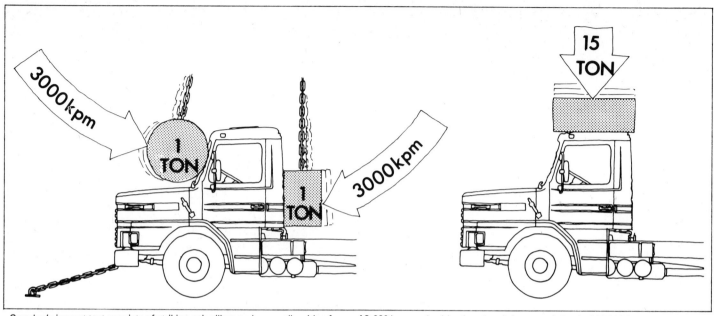

Sweden's impact test consists of striking cab pillars and rear walls with a force of 3,000 kpm and subjecting the roof to a static load of 15,000 kg.

covered a great deal of important ground over both decades, which is reflected in the product.

'Our goal from the safety viewpoint can be summarized in three central concepts,' he said. These were: safe and reliable function, which permitted fast and correct manoeuvering even in critical situations; greatest possible ride comfort and driver convenience, which prevented fatigue and facilitated concentration on driving and the surrounding traffic; and use of devices to reduce the effects of damage when an accident occured. In other words — function, comfort and protection.

A fundamental safety factor was the design and selection of materials with adequate safety margins. This rule, developed throughout the 1960s, applied first and foremost to all components which were directly concerned with road safety. These included axles and springs, king-pins on the front axles, hubs and wheels, bearings and wheel attachment devices. Of equal importance were all components in the steering system.

These included a number of levers, links and ball-joints.

Essential in the design of all such parts was that they should deform instead of fracture if exposed to excessive loads such as might occur in a collision or running off the road into a ditch. The same applied to all components in the braking system. Here, too, the dimensions of all parts needed to be designed to allow a good safety margin.

It was not possible in practice, he said, to give a truck-trailer combination of 30-40 tons the same kind of acceleration as a passenger car weighing between 1 and 1½ tons; but the largest engines developing a maximum of between 250 and 350 bhp and exhibiting extremely good torque characteristics nevertheless did enable such vehicles to maintain a good and steady speed, even when carrying heavy loads.

A powerful engine also gave the vehicle good hill-climbing ability, which helped prevent it from holding up other traffic

The cab-strength tests operated during the 1960s and 1970s have proved a big selling point for Swedish vehicles. These pictures show tests on the T cab being conducted at the Swedish Institute of Materials Testing in Alnarp, where type approval certificates are issued.

Instrument panel and control layout of a right-hand-drive LB76 cab.

on uphill gradients. As a basis for comparison, a vehicle with a power-to-weight ratio of 6 hp per ton driving up a long gradient with a constant incline of 5 per cent, for instance, could maintain a steady speed of approximately 15 mph (24 km/h). Under the same conditions, but with the power-to-weight ratio changed to 8 hp per ton, 20 mph (31 km/h) could be maintained, and with 10 hp per ton not less than 25 mph (40 km/h). More powerful engines thus gave heavy vehicles a far better chance of matching the general traffic rhythm in hilly country.

In order to utilize the available engine power, even on poor road surfaces and on slippery roads, axle loading on the

31

driving axle or axles had to be sufficiently high. The lowest value recommended was 25-30 per cent of the service weight on the driving wheels. He pointed out that to ensure a good traction even at low axle loadings, Scania trucks were accordingly fitted with a differential lock as standard.

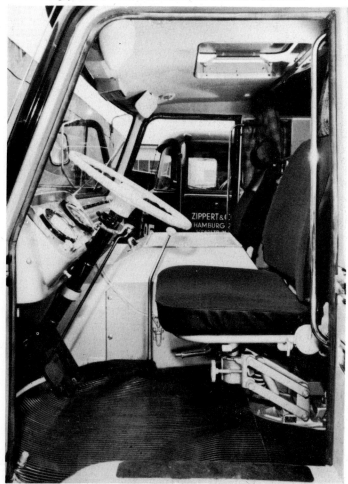

The interior of the LB76 cab showing the adjustment mechanism for the driver's seat.

In truck-trailer combinations requiring a three-axle tractive unit, the driving wheel loading might be lower than desirable if the bogie consisted of one driving and one trailing axle. In difficult situations, such as when starting on a hill, the drive-axle loading could then be temporarily increased with a bogie lift. In difficult and arduous driving conditions, a tandem-driven tractive unit was recommended.

Articulated vehicles were favoured where manoeuvrability was a main requirement, but the truck and drawbar-trailer combination, which was common in Sweden and on the Continent generally, tracked better when cornering and in addition had less tendency to jack-knife on over-braking (lorries and drawbar-trailers were the rule in Sweden in the 1960s, but a shift to artics was clearly discernible in the 1970s). Good stability, even at high speeds and on winding roads, was an important safety requirement. This could be satisfied by means of carefully designed understeering with properly damped springs and, where necessary, anti-roll bars.

With high-loaded vehicles a suspension design incorporating anti-roll characteristics counteracted the lateral displacement of the centre of gravity when cornering, and consequently increased the margin of safety against rolling over. It also counteracted 'snaking' and improved the feeling of safety.

When it came to satisfying safety requirements, the various measures adopted often overlapped. A typical example was power steering. A good power steering combined fast and precise reaction with a high degree of comfort and easy operation. This was of great importance in critical traffic situations in general, and in the case of potentially dangerous situations in particular, such as when a front wheel got stuck in a rut or ran into a soft shoulder. If it should be necessary to utilize the full capacity of the power steering in such a situation, the effort required by the steering wheel would still not be greater than about 18 lb. An ordinary manual steering system with normal gearing would require about 180 lb at the wheel to give the same steering result.

Should any fault arise in the servo of the steering system, the mechanical steering gear was retained as a safety reserve. In designing and building the steering system it was therefore necessary to ensure that the steering wheel effort, in normal

The Scania LB76 was powered by either the naturally aspirated D11 R03 engine producing 190 bhp, or the turbocharged DS11 R03, the output of which was initially rated at 220 bhp, a figure which was raised to 240 bhp in November 1964 and to 260 bhp in March 1967. Initially, Scania's own five-speed gearbox was fitted as standard, with the alternative of a splitter box based on the five-speed design. Scania's 10-speed synchronized gearbox was a further option from April 1964. Power steering, dual-circuit air brakes and an air-operated differential lock were standard fitments. Manufactured between January 1963 and February 1968, the LB76 had a gross vehicle weight of 16.5 tons and the LBS76 a gvw of 21/22 tons. The picture on the right is of a 1964 model.

A 1964-model LB76 road tanker with a two-axled drawbar trailer.

driving, was well within the limits of what a person could handle, even without the aid of the servo.

Brakes were equally important for driving safety. Most modern heavy trucks, John Rönnhult pointed out, used direct-acting air brakes. The driver had only to regulate the air pressure as required with the aid of a light foot-operated valve. Scania's air system was divided into two independent circuits for the foot brake. In addition, a third circuit was provided for the spring-type parking and emergency brake. Together, these circuits provided a wide margin of safety in the event of damage or leakage in any part of the system. Even if a fault should occur on both foot brake circuits, the emergency brake still remained operative.

Another important factor as regards safety was the adaptation of braking power to the total weight of the vehicle. High braking power with a good safety margin and short application times reduced the stopping distances. The ability of the brakes to withstand heat was an important link in the safety chain. If overheating occured, braking power might be reduced to a dangerous level and give rise to fading.

For this reason, every type of vehicle was subjected to special fade tests.

Brakes were heated-up in a standardized severe-braking programme. Braking power after this test should not fall off by more than 20 per cent. A similar testing programme in respect of water facing ensured that adequate braking power was retained even when the brakes were thoroughly soaked.

Additional safety devices were provided for trucks towing a trailer. The trailer had a separate braking circuit and a compressed air tank of its own. Should the trailer break free and the brake lines be broken, the trailer brakes would be automatically applied. A safety valve also ensured that the braking system of the tractive unit was not emptied through the broken line.

In Sweden, load-sensing brake valves which automatically regulated brake pressure to the axles in proportion to axle loadings were a prescribed fitment on all heavy vehicles. This device was of great importance for directional stability under emergency braking and for preventing 'swing-out' or 'jack-knifing' of the trailer or semi-trailer.

Two trucks from the T range on test at Södertälje, and tackling the water splash (opposite page) and one of the rough-road sections (above).

Several other designs were under development and would be in production within a few years (this has since happened as a result of the introduction of Scania's own anti-lock braking system).

An LB76 with two-axled semi-trailer fitted with the distinctive spherical cement tanks made by the Swedish Interconsull company unloading into a silo.

Speaking about Scania's synchromesh gearbox design philosophy, he pointed out that full synchronization of all gears, even for the heaviest trucks, ensured fast and convenient gear-changing with low gear-lever effort. This was an important safety factor in critical situations, he stressed.

Fully automatic transmissions would, in the future, give a further contribution to safe and easy operation on certain types of goods vehicles. (In mentioning this he obviously anticipated the announcement of Scania's own automatic box on the SBA111 and SBA111T cross-country models).

John Rönnhult also stressed — predictably — the importance for road safety of good visibility, good lighting and cab protection.

Scania's engine development work in the 1960s emphasised the company's interest in turbocharging. As already mentioned, the original turbocharger was a Brown Boveri unit, and this was used for much of the 1950s. Then a switch was made to British-built Holset units, different models of which were used throughout the 1960s and until 1972, when AiResearch units were fitted for the first time.

An interesting point here is that, before Holset was acquired by Cummins, in 1973, Holset and KKK both manufactured under licence from Schwitzer and, therefore, split the market between them into EEC and non-EEC countries. As a result Scania's factory in Zwolle in The Netherlands received KKK units which were identical — with certain exceptions — to the Holset units fitted by Södertälje. A number of substantial improvements have been made in turbocharger technology since the 1950s, pointers to which are the percentage increases in power output from turbocharging (more than 100 per cent more turbocharged power today than in the 1950s) and in the 'between services' life — a service was reckoned to be required at 180,000 miles in the 1950s whereas today it is virtually not required at all.

As for longevity, a Scania study of field tests of its DS14 engine has revealed that at least 90 per cent of the turbochargers completed 300,000 km of service without any failure and some returned as much as 500,000 km.

One of the interesting features of the early-1960s was the agreement with Mack Trucks in the USA for the supply of 140 bhp six-cylinder D8 engines for fitment in Macks. This was one outward sign of the considerable co-operation on technical matters between Mack and Scania, which went back to the immediate postwar period. It was an on-going relationship, too; when Mack placed its biggest order ever in 1969 for 1,770 engines, mostly DS8s, it brought the number of engines then taken by Mack to about 5,000. The 1979 US registration figures reveal that 500 Mack trucks in that year were fitted with Scania engines.

Towards the end of 1962, Scania introduced its model 56 and 76 truck series, the former bonneted and the latter in both normal and forward-control form. The LB76, as the forward-control model was designated, was the hope for the future as it was mainly designed and produced for the Continental market.

The LB76 was accordingly unveiled at the Brussels Show in 1963. It was offered with the then new D-series engine, the D11, which in naturally aspirated form produced a maximum power output of 190 bhp or, when turbocharged as the DS11,

220 bhp. The truck was fitted with air brakes all-round, three-line in the tractor unit version, power-steering, an air-operated differential lock and a mechanical multi-stage parking brake.

The basic nomenclature used by Scania is explained in the table accompanying this chapter. However, it is appropriate to underline the fact that the L-series were bonneted models and the LB-series were forward-control designs. Otherwise, the specification of an L76 was very similar to the LB76.

Although the L56 bonneted design had appeared in 1962, it was realised that there was a gap in the market between the 56 and 76 models, and in 1963 the L66 was introduced to plug this hole. It was not until the beginning of 1965, however, that a light version of the bonneted series, the L36, made its debut to satisfy a market need in the 8 to 12 tons gross weight class. Although this carried the L designation it was in fact a semi-forward-control vehicle, fitting either a D5 engine developing 95 bhp or a DS5 turbocharged power unit with a

The L76 six-wheeler was intended for rough, tough applications and it stood up to them well.

The L76 model as produced in the 1960s and shown here with a rock-hauling dumper body, one of the most successful models.

power rating of 120 bhp.

In the meantime, the L-series has been uprated — the L56 to 13 tons, the L66 to 15.2 tons, the L76 to 16 tons, the LS76 to 21.3 tons and the LT76 to 22.5 tons — by the fitment of higher weight capacity axles. The LB76 and LBS76 were uprated, too, to 16.5 tons and 22 tons, respectively, again by fitting uprated axles.

It is worth noting that the emphasis was still on bonneted designs. Things were, however, changing — a shift to forward-control was already desirable to satisfy European market demands. Scania was also starting to make major components to conform to the standards set by the Common Market countries. The needs of international haulage had likewise begun to make themselves felt, and a gearbox to meet these needs made its appearance. This was the G670 five-speed box with splitter to give 10 forward speeds. It was,

however, a versatile unit, being equipped with a power take-off and so being suitable for use on tippers, tankers, mixers and similar vehicles. Another 'European vehicle' development at this time — 1964 — included a 16 ton bogie to meet Continental standards.

One of the most significant, and difficult, periods for Scania was the build-up to Höger day in 1967. 'Höger' means 'right' in Swedish, and September 3, 1967, was the day the Swedish Government had designated for the switch from driving on the left to driving on the right. At this time, Sweden was the only country with left-hand traffic and a dry-land connection with other Continental countries with right-hand traffic. The five other drive-on-the-left countries — Britain, Ireland, Iceland, Cyprus and Malta — are all islands.

A massive national publicity campaign preceded the move to educate the public, especially drivers. For Scania, it meant extensive changes in production methods and models produced, with buses affected far more than trucks for it involved the total reconstruction of the nation's bus fleet. Virtually all the existing vehicles had their doors on the left side only and these had to be rebuilt to include passenger doors to the right. The task was complicated by the fact that a number of buses in use had their entrance doors ahead of the front axles; on these it was also necessary to move the driver's position. In comparison, truck conversion was no problem. The most extensive task which faced the Swedes, generally, stemmed from the changes required to road layout and traffic control. Drivers, of course, had to be educated to cope with right-hand-side driving, and one of the ways the Swedish authorities used to ease things was to restrict the licensing of new drivers until after the change. It is estimated that the changeover cost 600m Swedish crowns, of which 260m stemmed from converting buses and tramcars and 60m from rebuilding other vehicles.

This is something of a divergence from the Scania product, but it does illustrate what a massive problem Scania had to cope with, yet it coped successfully, at a time when it was having to develop vehicles to meet new needs and growing international competition.

The year 1965 marked the half-way stage in the decade, and so Scania paused to look at what had been achieved. In the

A vehicle transporter with a difference, carrying no fewer than six truck chassis. Hauled by an LB76, the outfit consists of an artic hauling a second semi-trailer fitted with a dolly.

previous 10 years production had more than doubled from 3,638 trucks and buses in 1954 to more than 10,400 in 1965, of which 60 per cent were exported. The manufacturing complex at Södertälje now employed around 4,200 people, not counting those in the car franchise division.

Perhaps one of the most significant moves in terms of future sales came in 1966 when Scania unveiled a new all-steel normal-control cab. This remedied many of the 'dated' features of the existing cab, being of much stronger construction and having the cab part integrated with the front of the vehicle. It didn't have the old one's rattles and was better sealed against the elements and well sound-insulated. Deeper side windows contributed to improved all-round visibility, as did the insertion of rear corner windows and one let into the panel in the back of the cab.

This cab was fitted on the normal-control versions of the 76-series, which was updated at this time, the first examples coming off the production line in March, 1967. This vehicle had the uprated DS11 engine, delivering 171 bhp on the DIN

scale. It also had a modified gearbox with more robust gears and a stronger propeller-shaft. The same cab was fitted in 1968 on the company's series 80, 85 and 110 models.

The same year saw the introduction of new forward-control designs which, with other versions yet to come, were to consolidate Scania's position in the European market. These were the LB110 and LBS110 models with gross weights of 17 and 22.5 tons, respectively. The larger LBT110, with tandem-drive bogie, was to follow in 1968 and a smaller one, the LB80, in 1969. Yet a further smaller, but more powerful version, the LB85, followed hard on its heels. Using many of the chassis components of the 110 models, it was powered by the DS8 engine developing 202 bhp on the DIN scale.

The year 1969 was to be a bumper one for new launches, however, for in September three more models in this LB series made their appearance. These were the LB140, LBS140 and LBT140, all powered by a new 14-litre V8 engine, the DS14, developing 350 bhp at 2,300 rpm and a torque of 892 lb ft at 1,400 rpm.

An LBS76 three-axled TIR vehicle hauling a drawbar trailer in wintery conditions.

Below left, a Scania diagram showing the merits of turbocharged engines in vehicles used in mountainous countries. Below, a graph, also produced by Scania, to emphasize that a turbocharged engine emits much less smoke than a normally aspirated power unit.

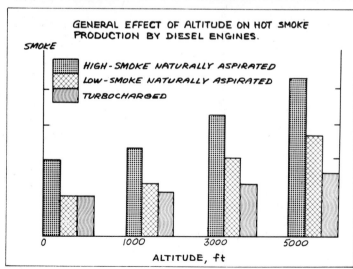

GENERAL EFFECT OF ALTITUDE ON HOT SMOKE PRODUCTION BY DIESEL ENGINES.

SMOKE

- HIGH-SMOKE NATURALLY ASPIRATED
- LOW-SMOKE NATURALLY ASPIRATED
- TURBOCHARGED

ALTITUDE, ft

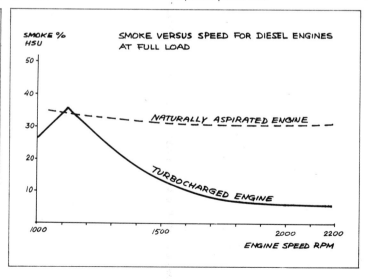

SMOKE % HSU

SMOKE VERSUS SPEED FOR DIESEL ENGINES AT FULL LOAD

NATURALLY ASPIRATED ENGINE

TURBOCHARGED ENGINE

ENGINE SPEED RPM

40

Popular for tipping operations as a short-wheelbase vehicle, this LB76 is shown releasing its load of rock.

Basic Scania nomenclature

Scania has three basic engine sizes and the piston displacement of the engines is used as the series designations of the chassis models; this has been so since the D-series engines were completed.

The three basic engines are the 8-litre, 11-litre and 14-litre units, all of which are available in turbocharged and naturally aspirated versions.

The smallest engine size (the D8 and the turbocharged DS8) is included in the range of trucks designated 81 and 86. The range of trucks with the intermediate size of engine — the D11 and DS11 — is known as the 111 series, and the largest engine — the D14 and DS14 — powers the 171 and 176 range of trucks, and the latest series, which are designated 82, 112 and 142.

About 150 different versions of vehicles are available in each series, counting the wheelbase alternatives available. Most models are supplied in both right and left-hand drive form.

Forward-control (cab-over-engine) trucks are designated LB (two-axle), LBS (three-axle 6 x 2) and LBT (three-axle 6 x 4). The corresponding bonnet-type trucks are designated L, LS and LT. Where LK is used in the designation, the vehicle is forward-control, but built with the front axle set forward to increase the wheelbase, reduce front overhang and increase the axle-centre to back-of-cab length.

The best sellers in the 1960s — the L75, L56, L76, LB76 and L36.

Although launched in May 1958, the L75 can be said to have taken Scania into the 1960s because it was built until January 1963. It was the first to fit the then new D-series engine. This was the D10 R01 which, in naturally aspirated form, produced 165 bhp. When installed as a turbocharged unit — the DS10 R01 — it produced 205 bhp. This vehicle had features which stamped it as being in advance of its time, including Bendix-Westinghouse air braking, power-steering and a differential lock.

Offered in a variety of wheelbase forms from 3.4m to 5.4m, the gross weight range was from 13 tons to 15.5 tons, with the six-wheeled LS75 ranging from 17 tons to 19.75 tons gross and a tandem-axle model — the LT75 — grossing 22 tons. Both these three-axled vehicles had the same power train as the four-wheeler.

The L56 was introduced in November 1962 and was then built until February 1968. This had the D8 R01 engine producing 180 bhp and the G650-2 five-speed synchromesh gearbox. Built for operation at 12.6 tonnes gross vehicle weight, the permutation of wheelbases available ranged from 3.4 to 5.4m. Air brakes and power-steering were standard fitments. The lightweight LS56 six-wheeler had a gross weight rating of 16.6 tons.

January 1963 marked the introduction of the L76 and L76 Super models. They were offered with the 190 bhp D11 R01 naturally-aspirated diesel as standard, with the DS11 R01 turbocharged model rated at 220 bhp as an alternative. This engine was the subject of two revised power upratings — to 240 bhp in November 1964 and 260 bhp in 1967. The standard gearbox was initially the G660 five-speed synchromesh, but the 10-speed splitter and range-change versions became available in 1967.

The wheelbase options ranged from 3.4m to 5.4m and the gross weight ratings from 13.15 to 15.7 tons.

The LS76 and the LS76 Super had the same engine and gearbox options as the L76 and L76 Super, but ranged in rated gross weights from 17 tons to 20 tons and later (in 1964) to 21 tons. The tandem-axled LT76 Super had a gross weight rating of 22.25 tons initially, but this was uprated to 22.5 tons in 1964.

In April 1963 and November 1964 two new Scania bonneted model ranges appeared, the L66 and the L36. The L66 was fitted with the D8 R02, rated at 140 bhp, which was matched initially with the G650-2 five-speed synchromesh gearbox, and later with the L670 and the G671 10-speed unit.

The L36, along with the L36 Super, were the smallest models in the Scania range, fitting the D5 R01 95 bhp power unit or the DS5 R01 turbocharged unit, which had an output of 125 bhp. They were rated initially to operate at 10.5 tons and then, from November 1965, at 11.2 tons.

January, 1963, saw the introduction of the LB76 range, which included the LB76 and the LB76 Super, the LBS76 and the LBS76 Super. The forward-control LB76 introduction marked the first move by Scania away from bonneted to forward-control designs.

Apart from the cab difference and the ancillary effects of forward-control rather than a bonneted design, there was no great difference from the L76 except that gross weight on the LB76 four-wheelers was 16.5 tons and 21 tons (from April 1964, 22 tons) on the LBS76 and LBS76 Super. Engine and gearbox details were exactly the same, and wheelbase options were more limited, from 3.45m to 5m on the LB76 and LBS76. Air brakes and power-steering were standard.

Chapter 3

Defence role and the models of the 1970s

Only passing reference has been made to Scania's military-vehicle involvement, but obviously the company has had a continuous role in this sector. In the 1960s and early-1970s Scania's best-seller for defence use was the smallest model produced, the L50, which was introduced in 1965. A number of these were fitted with special bodywork for preventive maintenance, being operated throughout the year, even in Sweden's severe winter weather, as mobile workshops. Others were fitted with general transport bodies for a variety of uses.

One of the main projects developed during the 1960s was a large cross-country vehicle for, among other uses, hauling medium/heavy field artillery. Called the Ant-Eater, but designated the LA82, this was designed mainly as a tractor unit, but was also used as an ammunition carrier. Additionally, it was adapted for a variety of other purposes, being used, for example, as the basis for a mobile crane by the Swedish army's engineers and as a heavy recovery vehicle.

A project due for completion in the 1970s, which was also worked on in the 1960s by Scania with the Swedish Defence Material Administration, was the task of producing cross-country vehicles. These were handed over to the Swedish forces for testing and evaluation in 1971.

After intensive testing under both winter conditions and over snow-free ground, two main types went into production, a 4 x 4 version designated the SBA111 and the other, a 6 x 6, to be known as the SBAT111. The two-axle version was developed as a tractor for light artillery and for the general transport of equipment, while the three-axle version was intended as a heavy artillery tractor and load-carrier.

Built for carrying capacities of 4.5 tons and 6 tons, respectively, with the vehicles towing trailers with gross weights of 6 tons and 12 tons, both vehicles had a high specific engine output. The two-axle Scania SBA111 was fitted with a type D11 naturally aspirated diesel and the SBAT111 was powered by the turbocharged DS111.

Scania also developed a fully automatic gearbox of the split-torque type, in which two-thirds of the power was transmitted mechanically to restrict power losses in the hydraulic section to a minimum. The main gearbox had six speeds, three hydraulic and three mechanical, and the transfer box had two ratios, one for cross-country operation and the other for highway use.

Designed specifically for good cross-country performance, the trucks could climb gradients of up to 60 per cent (30 degrees) and negotiate water up to 80 cm in depth. Clearance angles of 40 degrees at the rear and 45 degrees at the front, with the ability to tilt more than 25 degrees sideways without overturning, gave them maximum mobility in difficult conditions. This was enhanced by a turning radius of 8.9 metres for the two-axle vehicle, and 9.0 metres for the three-axle machine. Needless to say, the vehicles were built for operation in the worst type of winter conditions, and equipped accordingly.

By the early-1970s, apart from having the updated cab

Scania's SBA111 cross-country vehicles, which first went on trial in 1971, can negotiate hills with a gradient of up to 60 per cent, operate at a lateral tilt of 25 degrees and tackle water up to 80 cm deep. They are equipped with automatic transmission.

On the L140 and LS140, introduced in the early-1970s, the engine can be entirely exposed to provide good accessibility for maintenance by raising the plastic engine cover.

The engine cowl tipped forward to expose the V8 and to emphasize the relationship between this and the forward-control cab of the LB80 from which it was derived.

from 1966, Scania's bonneted models had had only detail changes made in the previous 10 years, so by 1972 changes were obviously necessary. In March of that year the L140 and LS140 were announced, with the gross weight of the two-axle L140 being 19.5 tons and that of the three-axle LS140, 23 tons. However, as Scania pointed out, permitted gross weights differed according to national legislation. Within the Common Market countries, the L140 was available in four wheelbases — 3.8, 4.2, 4.6 and 5.4 metres. In the case of the LS140 the alternatives were 4.2 and 5.4 metres.

Designed especially for use in heavy and exacting conditions, such as forestry and site operations, as well as comparable heavy transport under arduous operating conditions this new range featured a new all-steel cab based on the LB80 design. Made of glassfibre-reinforced plastic, the

bonnet hinged at the front end to allow the whole of the engine to be exposed when the bonnet was tilted forward to an angle of 70 degrees.

A high standard of comfort for the driver was the aim behind a number of innovations. To achieve a low noise level it was lined with a sound-insulating material, and instruments had been centrally located in front of the driver. The driver's seat was adjustable to the required position and the springing was also adjustable to suit the driver's weight. A three-point suspension for the cab ensured that the driver did not bump about through road surface shocks being transmitted.

The DS14 V8 was the principal power unit offered and it was matched with the Scania GR 860 range-change gearbox, a five-speed gearbox with high and low ratios, the high or low ratio being selected by means of a switch on the gear-lever. A

Above left, a picture revealing the attention paid to providing good driver access to the cab of L140 and LS140 vehicles. Above, the driving position in the LS140 and the grouping of the controls and instruments.

An example of the Scania LS140 introduced in 1972 operating with a three-axled trailer at 50 tons gross train weight.

The functional instrument panel of the LB111 series launched in 1975 with non-reflecting instruments and controls grouped a convenient distance from the driver. A two-spoke steering wheel aids instrument visibility.

standards in vehicles. Scania's design reflected this, and in a 'de Luxe' version, particularly intended for international operation, the cab was lined with velour fabric and a fitted carpet covered the floor and engine casing. A shelf above the windscreen supported a built-in radio and stereo cassette tape recorder, and there was provision for a two-way radio.

The colour scheme within the driver's field of sight was subdued so as to make it less tiring on the eyes. The instrument panel was of a functional design with a matt black finish, all materials used being of impact-absorbing material and instrument dials were of a non-reflecting type. Controls were grouped in front of the driver to ensure that important information was conveyed quickly, all instrument pointers being of a distinctive colour. A two-spoke steering wheel was fitted so as to give the driver a clear view of the instruments.

Anatomically designed, sprung and adjustable seats for both the driver and passenger were upholstered with a velour type of material, and the edges were reinforced with fabric-backed plastic. An extremely quiet cab interior was obtained

blocking device was featured to prevent changing from the high to the low range when the speed was excessively high. A single-reduction hypoid rear axle was the standard specification, but hub reduction units could be delivered as optional equipment.

This generation of bonneted models was rounded off in January 1975 with the Scania LT145, a new tandem-drive design built for ultra-heavy operations, particularly as an artic for machinery transport. Accordingly, it was fitted with a 7 tonne front axle, the rear bogie, equipped with hub reduction, being of 23 tonnes load rating. It was powered by the DS14 V8 engine and the Scania GR 860 gearbox, but with a different clutch to that fitted on the lighter bonneted models, in this case with a new type of hydraulic power assistance designed to improve pull-away performance under heavy load.

At the same time as the LT145 made its debut, Scania unveiled a new normal-control cab. This was the period of the boom in transport to the Middle East, which encouraged new

Easy access with anti-slip steps and good handholds are important features of the cab of the new T range.

The Scania de luxe cab of 1975 was equipped to provide maximum comfort on international journeys. The whole of the cab was lined with velour fabric, and the floor and engine casing covered with fitted carpet. A radio and stereo tape recorder were built into the shelf above the screen and many other aids were provided to improve the comfort and ease the work of the driver.

It was also equipped with lined storage compartments under the seats, that under the driver's seat being provided with a bottle stand! Another important feature was a lockable document compartment on the engine casing.

An extra sun vizor was fitted above the left-hand door, and the two external main rear-view mirrors were electrically heated. The cab had curtains which could be drawn across the doors and windscreen, and pockets made of netting were provided for the storage of small items. A slightly less luxurious sleeper cab version was also offered, along with a shorter, normal day cab.

Yet another development unveiled in January 1975 was the LB80 Automatic — a distribution truck with fully automatic transmission developed by Scania. The new gearbox — designated type GA 651 — had four forward speeds and one reverse. A feature of it was that it provided the driver with the option of limiting the gear-changing; by use of a lever connected to the box, the higher speeds could be blocked so that automatic changing was limited to the low-speed ratios.

by the extensive use of insulating materials in the walls and doors and of thick insulating felt/rubber matting to cover the floor and engine casing. The insulation also protected against heat.

Because the 'de Luxe' cab was intended for living in as well as driving, it was, of course, a sleeper cab with one or two folding bunks — measuring 700 mm x 1900 mm (2ft 3½in x 6ft 2in) — being provided, together with a portable wardrobe.

The most robust and powerful Scania model before the introduction of the 146 and the T series was the L145. Equipped with the 375 bhp V8 engine, this vehicle was designed for really heavy work or long-distance duties.

This Scania LB140 tractor unit, which went on the road in 1974, is plated for 70 tons and is powered by the 335 bhp 14-litre Scania diesel, which drives through a GR 860 10-speed all-synchromesh gearbox.

One of the new features of the 1975 Scania 111 was the fitment of a more powerful 296 bhp diesel engine.

A V8-powered Scania LB141 tractor unit seen here hauling a tri-axle semi-low-loading tilt trailer.

The sound insulation treatment applied to the forward-control cabs was also to be found in the LB80 Automatic to give an interior noise level at maximum acceleration no higher than 75 dB(A).

This in effect was Scania's basic range for the remainder of the 1970s, although there were one or two important detail developments yet to come. Undoubtedly the most important of these was the launch in 1976 of an economy version of its DS14 engine. The philosophy behind this is described elsewhere in this book, but basically the concept was to offer a fuel-efficient engine rated at 385 bhp, but low-revving. Thus, when cruising at a steady 70 kmh, the 1,400 rpm engine speed enabled maximum benefit to be derived from the low specific fuel consumption figure of 155g/bhph.

Apart from this, Scania developed its own anti-lock braking system for heavy vehicles; introduced an air-suspension system designed for tankers, container carriers and vehicles intended for use in distribution systems where demountable bodies had to be mounted or dismounted; made parabolic springs available to a greater degree on certain models; and made detail improvements to its gearboxes.

In summary, the Scanias of the 1970s consisted of the

This LB81 tractor unit is towing a Crane Fruehauf tipping trailer with a capacity of 40.4 cubic yards at 32 tons gross, the UK maximum weight limit. It is powered by the Scania DS8 7.78-litre six-cylinder turbocharged engine which produces 205 bhp at 2,400 rpm and has the GS 760 10-speed all-synchromesh gearbox.

The Scania 141 and 146 models, introduced in the second half of the 1970s, are equipped with a high-output V8 engine developing 375 bhp nett. These vehicles are designed for really heavy work, as in this instance, where a 146 is shown hauling a machinery-carrying low-loader.

widest spread of models yet. Here's how they lined up as the decade drew to a close:

The Scania 81 had a relatively light frame and axle equipment, designed for duties such as short-haul distribution and similar applications. Engine options (DIN ratings) were the DS8m, developing 151 kW (205 bhp), and the D8, developing 120 kW (163 bhp). All models were available with a five-speed or 10-speed gearbox. Three alternative rear-axle ratios were offered. The L81 version was bonneted and available in four wheelbase alternatives. The LB81 was a forward-control unit, offered with six optional wheelbases, ranging from short tractors with a wheelbase of 3.1m (10.2ft) up to trucks with a wheelbase of 5.4m (17.7ft). The LB81

Automatic had a four-speed fully automatic transmission.

The Scania 86 had a more robust frame and higher-rated axle equipment than the 81 model and was designed for more arduous transport duties, including off-road operation. The bonneted L86 was a two-axle truck and the LS86, also bonneted, was a three-axle unit, the latter being available for a gross weight of 23 tons. The LB86 and LBS86 were the equivalent normal-control models.

The Scania 111, designed for both short-haul and long-distance transport, was powered by the turbocharged DS11 engine, developing 218 kW (296 bhp), again on the DIN scale. The standard gearbox was a 10-speed, (five with splitter) fully synchromesh unit. Three rear-axle options were available,

Scania's largest engine, the DS14, is a compact V8 design and has a low normal running speed so as to increase engine life and reduce fuel consumption.

one featuring hub reductions and being designed for extra-arduous duties. A wide variety of alternative equipment — sleeper cabs, parabolic springs and wheel alternatives — was offered on this range to suit particular needs. Models in this range were used for solo operation at gross vehicle weights from 16.5 tons, and as tractors for hauling semi-trailers or drawbar trailers at gross weights of 50 tons or above.

The bonneted L111 was a two-axle truck, and the LS111, 6 x 2, a three-axle unit available with bogie lift on the trailing axle. The LT111 series was a three-axle truck with two driven rear axles (6 x 4), with individual differential locks and a differential lock for the whole bogie. The normal-control models were designated LB111 (two-axle), LBS111 (three-axle 6 x 2 with bogie lift) and LBT111 (three-axle 6 x 4), but

Although Scania offers a twin-steering eight-wheeler in certain overseas markets, notably Britain, this tanker for BP is something of a rarity in Sweden, where such vehicles are only used for very specific tasks. Eight-wheelers were really a late-1970s development from Scania, and when used in Sweden drawbar trailers are often hauled by them, as in the case of this container transporter.

The LB81 has a lighter chassis than the LB86 and is designed primarily for distribution work. Engine options are the 120 kW (163 bhp) D8 and the 224 kW (205 bhp) DS8-01.

The Scania LB86, which has more robust chassis frame, springs and axles than the lighter LB81 and is built for more arduous transport and higher gross vehicle weights. The same engine options apply, however, namely the D8 or the DS8-01, offering 163 and 205 bhp, respectively.

Designed for intensive short-haul duties as well as long-distance transport, this Scania 111 can be fitted with either the turbocharged DS11-01 engine, which develops 206 kW (280 bhp), or the DS11-02, which produces 224 kW (305 bhp) nett.

otherwise were similar in specification to the bonneted models. A high-specification 'de luxe' long-distance cab was offered on these vehicles.

Scania 140s and 145s were both equipped with the Scania V8 engine, developing 257 kW (350 bhp) on the DIN scale. They were designed for truly heavy transport, or long-distance duties in which high average speeds and a high transport capacity were vital features. The gearbox on both models was a 10-speed fully synchromesh unit with an extra-low bottom gear (13.51:1) for starting at a high gross weight and from difficult positions. A high engine output and matched rear axle ratio were designed to reduce the need for gear-changing.

The bonneted L140 was a two-axle truck, the LS140 was the three-axle 6 x 2 version, and the LT145 the tandem bogie-driven 6 x 4 (with bogie lift on the trailing axle). The forward-control LB140 and the three-axle LBS140 normal-control models were all DS14-powered and built for both long-distance and heavy short-haul transport. The LBT140 three-

Fitted with a Neville Charrold aluminium alloy body, this LBT86 6 × 4, built for operation at 24 tons gross weight, was shown at the British tipper exhibition in April 1980.

axle version with tandem-driven bogie had a four-spring bogie with each rear axle mounted on two separate springs, with linkage evenly distributing the force between the two driving axles when the vehicle was driven on an uneven surface.

So to the 1980s, and Scania was again not slow to make moves to carry its designs through, perhaps, to the end of the century. A brand new range of bonneted models — the T range — made its debut in April, 1980.

The announcement of the T-range was significant because it replaced the L models, which basically had been in production for over 20 years, the L75 having been launched in 1958. The T stands for Torpedo, a common expression in Scandinavia for bonneted trucks. The range consists of medium-weight, heavy and extra-heavy models designated M, H and E, respectively.

There are two medium-weights — the T82M and T112M, both 4 x 2 designs. Seven configurations comprise the H-range. They are: T82H (4 x 2); T82H (6 x 2); T112H (4 x 2); T112H (6 x 2); T112H (6 x 4); T142H (4 x 2) and T142H (6 x 2). The E-range consists of the T112E (4 x 2), T112E (6 x 4) and T142E (6 x 4).

Engines used as power plants in the T programme are the latest models of the Scania 8-litre, 11-litre and 14-litre diesel engines, fitted, respectively, in the M, H and E models. None of these engines has been uprated to exceed its performance in

The Scania T142E 6 × 4 being used as a tractor for the movement of heavy construction equipment. The vehicle is capable of operating at weights of 100 to 150 tons.

previous models. Five engine power options are offered, with turbocharged and naturally aspirated versions of the 8-litre and 11-litre engines.

By combining five-speed or 10-speed gearboxes with a range of rear-axle gear ratios, vehicles can be specified to meet a variety of traction and road-speed requirements. New propeller shafts, rear-axle housings and other drive-line components offer a modular concept for different types of haulage operation.

Bonnet and cab have been standardized for manufacturing and service purposes, and are identical for all models in the programme. Gear-lever, pedal configuration and other controls have been redesigned and relocated, and similar design changes have been made to controls for the heating and ventilation systems, lights, differential lock and other important features, including the design and layout of instrument clusters. The new dashboard includes a completely new fusebox and relay bank with 'in-house electronics', and a system for integrating air conditions in the heating and ventilation system.

The 1980 Scania T142H is a 6 × 2 built for long-distance operation and features a two-bunk sleeper cab.

Fitted with the DS11 engine, the 1980 Scania T112H is a 6 × 2 built for medium and long-distance haulage.

The 1980 Scania T142E pictured here and on the jacket of this book with tipper bodywork is a 6 × 4 specially adapted for heavy-duty operations, primarily on poor roads.

The best sellers in the 1970s — the LB85 and LB110

March 1968 saw the introduction of a range which carried Scania not only into the 1970s, but virtually to the 1980s, the forward-control LB80 and LB110 models. Both of these had been preceded, however, by just one month, by new bonneted models; the L50, the L50 Super and the L80 and L80 Super.

The first two were built for operation at 12 tons gvw. They fitted the D5R01 diesel initially producing 95 bhp, then uprated to 105 bhp in naturally-aspirated form and to 120 bhp when turbocharged. The Scania five-speed gearbox was standard on all models which were offered in a choice of three wheelbases: 4.2, 4.8 and 5.4m.

The 140 bhp D8 R01 diesel (later to be uprated to 155 bhp and producing 190 bhp turbocharged) provided the power for the L80 and L80 Super models. Again the five-speed synchromesh gearbox was offered, but this was supplemented by the GS750 10-speed gearbox in 1971. These were the engine and gearbox options in the LB-series, and there were many common points to the specification including the fitment of power-steering, air brakes and an air-operated differential lock.

Wheelbases and gross laden weight ratings varied. Whereas the wheelbase options of the L80 ranged from 3.8m to 5.4m, those of the LB80 were from 3.05 to 5m, the L80 and the L80 Super being rated for operation at 14.7 tons and 15.5 tons, respectively, and the LB80 and LB80 Super at 15.5 tons and 16 tons.

The bonneted L85 and L85 Super models were also introduced in February 1968, but their forward-control LB counterparts did not come along until November of the same year. Built for a total weight of 16 tons in the case of the bonneted and 16.5 tons in the case of the forward-control designs, both ranges had the same power train specification, fitting the 190 bhp turbocharged DS8 R01 engine initially, but supplementing this in 1970 by the 155 bhp naturally-aspirated version. Scania's 10-speed G570 gearbox was fitted at first, and later the improved G572. Offered in wheelbases from 3.8m to 5.4m, the bonneted range was available in greater variety than the LB85 and the LB85 Super, which had just three wheelbase options of 3.4m, 4.2m and 5.0m.

What was to prove to be the most popular range of all, the LB110 series, made its debut in February 1968 alongside the L110. All the L110 and LB110 series were fitted with either the Scania D11 R01 engine rated at 190 bhp, or the turbocharged Scania DS11 R01A producing 260 bhp. Initially, the Scania 10-speed synchromesh unit in a variety of forms was the standard gearbox, but the five-speed unit was offered later. Wheelbases ranged from 3.4m to 5m in the case of forward-control, and 3.8m to 5.4m for the bonneted designs.

With the multi-wheelers, the LS110 six-wheeler was rated at 22 tons gvw and the LBS110 at 22.5 tons. When the LBT110 Super tandem six-wheeler made its debut in January 1969, however, the gross weight rating moved to 24.5 tons. The LB140 Super completed the range in July 1969 as a heavy-duty three-axled tractor unit, the Scania V8 power unit, the 350 bhp DS14 LB01 was introduced, matched with the Scania GR860 10-speed synchromesh gearbox.

Chapter 4

Södertälje — The quiet factory
that says it with flowers

The product-development programme at Scania in the 1960s and 1970s would not have been possible without extensive investment programmes in buildings, production equipment and methods.

The first substantial development in the 1960s in this direction was the construction in 1962 of a 20,000 m^2 parts centre. Then, in the following year, a start was made on the construction of a new frame assembly shop. This was a major project and it was not completed until 1965, being opened officially in the summer of that year.

In the mid-1960s, Scania's plant at Södertälje was extremely busy on the conversion of buses to the changeover to right-hand drive, but inevitably, once the changeover had been made, bus demand would fall. This was appreciated by the Scania management, and in the autumn of 1966 the first stage of a reorganization was completed with the manufacture of bodyworked buses being transferred to Katrineholm. This followed an agreement to purchase the plant there of bus bodybuilder Svenska Karossenverkstaderna. The move was completed by the beginning of 1968.

Explaining the move at the time, Gösta Nilsson, Scania's managing director, said that the expected decline in bus sales after the changeover to right-hand traffic offered an excellent opportunity to transfer the bus chassis manufacturing activity as it also freed production capacity for trucks in Södertälje, which was urgently needed to meet the rapid expansion in export demand.

A new central laboratory was completed in 1964, and construction work started on a vehicle proving ground adjacent to it. This test facility, featuring an extensive track which includes a number of punishingly steep gradients, bends, straights and surface variations, was opened officially in 1966 as part of Scania's 75 years' jubilee celebrations.

To coincide with the company's celebrations, on September 9, 1966, a new 100 million Swedish crowns investment programme was embarked upon. It included the construction of a new head office, a new plant for power and heating, the establishment of a plant at Lulea, in Northern Sweden, north of the arctic circle, and a new chassis construction hall at Södertälje.

The opening of the striking new office building in Södertälje, with its 10,000 m^2 of floor area, was one of the highlights of the jubilee celebrations, the modern building dominating the plant complex at Södertälje in its attractive lakeside setting. The new chassis assembly hall, covering a floor area of close on 50,000 m^2 (the building being 360m long by 132m wide) was the biggest part of the company's new investment and, when it came on stream in 1968, it was almost certainly the most advanced heavy truck plant in Europe.

Some of the features which impressed me when I visited it shortly after it had opened were the quietness, the spaciousness and the effort made by the management and workers together to make the place attractive to work in.

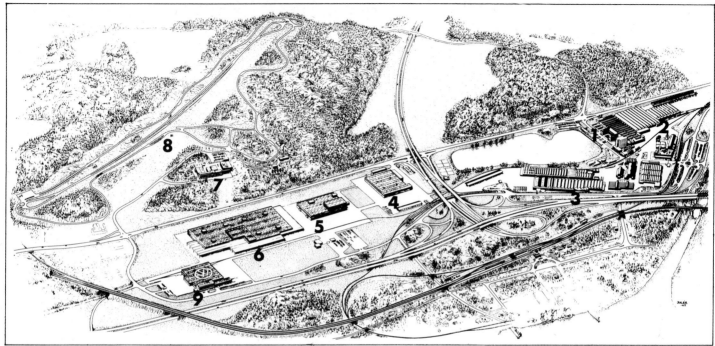

The Södertälje factory as it was in 1966. 1 — main offices; 2 — engine factory; 3 — bus factory; 4 — spare parts stores; 5 — frame factory; 6 — chassis assembly factory; 7 — development centre; 8 — test track; 9 — Volkswagen centre.

The quietness was no accident. Scania noise evaluation teams in 1968 had measured noise levels in every working area, plotting the decibel levels in each one throughout the plant. Then steps had been taken to reduce the noise to a minimum by the use of strategically positioned acoustic panels, setting up insulated noise barriers, adopting air-operated tools instead of electro-mechanical units, and a whole host of other ingenious devices.

Probably the most spectacular development in this noise-reduction programme was the development by Scania with Atlas Copco of air-operated 'nut runners'. Work started on this as early as 1966. Previously, Scania had relied mainly on impact wrenches for tightening nuts during assembly. In these machines, noise was generated by a number of sources — the tightening process itself was very noisy because of the

hammering, but the exhaust air from the air drive was also very disturbing. It was difficult to silence impact machines; by using special silencers, it was found that the sound level from the exhaust air could be reduced, but it was almost impossible to reduce the noise from the impact mechanism. In addition, because of the design of the impact wrench, it was not possible to maintain the necessary close tolerances on the tightening torque.

However, the new nut runner could be silenced simply by adding an exhaust silencer, or by diverting the exhaust air, or by mounting it in a sound-absorbent box. Comparative noise measurements showed clearly the advantages of the new nut runners as regards noise. As an example, in assembling brake drums on wheel hubs, the noise level was reduced from 100 dB(A) to 78 when the change was made from impact wrenches

Test-driving Scania's LS71 model of the 1950s. This example, being operated by the company's experimental department, was photographed in 1956.

A demonstration in 1956 of what happens in the event of servo blow-out and the effect of using power steering. The vehicle is an LS71.

These rotating nut-running machines developed by Scania and Atlas-Copco lack an impact mechanism and reduce noise level considerably inside the factory.

to the new nut runners. Measurements from the assembly of spring shackles showed 83 dB(A) for the new nut runner as against 105 for the older impact machine.

Working conditions were made more acceptable by having 'flower gardens' inside the factory, and even shops at which employees could buy such things as drinks, magazines and books.

From the production viewpoint the new chassis assembly hall had several outstanding features. One of these was the computer-controlled high-rise spare parts store, which was sited within the chassis building hall. Supplied by Westinghouse Electric Corporation in the USA, this had a storage capacity of up to 19,000 pallet loads of parts standing to 15m high. All parts from outside suppliers are the subject of a quality audit as they come from the goods inwards loading bays (strategically placed adjoining the store area) before being allowed into the storage system.

One of the most impressive features of Scania's production process is its high level of quality control. I remember

Proving work being undertaken on an F11 four-wheel-drive vehicle in 1949, well before the company had its own test track and surface-testing facilities.

Cross-country testing with an F11. Note the use of chains on both front and rear wheels.

Could you find worse natural test conditions? An L60 'ice-breaker' pictured below clearing the way on a road across a lake in 1955. Below right, Scania built its 10,000th post-World War Two truck for export in 1957, when it was pictured about to leave the line at Södertälje.

The chassis-assembly line at Södertälje with a row of forward-control vehicles nearing completion.

made, as already indicated, right back when the material or component first reached the company. With certain supplies a first requirement was a certificate based on the composition and strength of the material. A quality audit of components and materials involved rigorous testing with very tight tolerances. Testing for hardness in metal components, for example, was insisted on and if, say, a cylinder-head proved to have too soft a material — with a resulting risk of cracks developing after a period in use — the whole batch could be rejected.

Similarly, loading tests were carried out on a large proportion of every delivery of springs and, in addition, regular fatigue tests were executed. It was regarded as important that a spring bundle had the correct relationship between loading and deflection, for if the springs were different the vehicle would soon tend to lean over to one side. Continuous fatigue testing resulted in a knowledge of springs supplied. A total of 30-40,000 deflections in the rig used was expected. If a set of springs proved to have too short a life the

listening in 1970 to an impressive account by Bengt Bendelius, the head of SAAB-Scania's quality-control activities, at the Amsterdam Show.

As he rightly emphasized then, a customer has the right to expect that the vehicle he buys will fulfil his expectations, a basic condition of purchase being that a vehicle is not afflicted with defects that affect the operation or the life of the finished product.

This, of course, is the function of the quality-control activity, and it is worth taking a look at some of the areas that the company's quality-control inspectors examined before placing a yellow ticket on the windscreen to indicate that it was ready for delivery, for these procedures of the 1960s were a pointer to Scania's success in the 1970s. The system was based on a route-card, which followed the chassis from the start of assembly to the point when, fully assembled, it was driven on to a roller tester or on to the company's test track and then over to a checking line for final inspection.

Before use, detail items and sub-assemblies were subjected to a comprehensive checking procedure, the first check being

A bonneted L-series 140 in the final stages of assembly at Södertälje. Note the light working conditions on the assembly line.

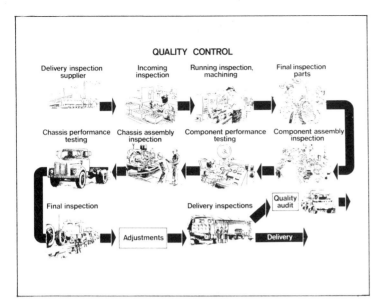

QUALITY CONTROL

Delivery inspection supplier → Incoming inspection → Running inspection, machining → Final inspection parts

Chassis performance testing ← Chassis assembly inspection ← Component performance testing ← Component assembly inspection

Final inspection → Adjustments → Delivery inspections → Quality audit → Delivery

Quality-control was of a high order at the Södertälje plant towards the end of the 1960s, when this diagram was prepared. Ten years later it was to be even more advanced.

Correct spring deflection characteristics have been regarded as important by Scania for many years. Here a spring is seen being tested in the 1960s for both loading and deflection qualities.

supplier was immediately contacted and asked to investigate and remedy.

Not all components are of metal, so Scania had an equally stringent control process for items made of other materials. Recognizing, for example, that a rubber coolant hose must not only tolerate large temperature variations, but must remain elastic at all temperatures, be oil-resistant, not age quickly and crack, and have specified form and dimensions, Scania checked the thermal capacity of the hose by cooling it to a temperature of about -40 degrees C and then compressing it to half its diameter. It was passed if no cracks appeared.

Weathering ability was checked by an ozone test, for ozone in the atmosphere affects rubber and causes it to crack. Accelerated ultra-violet tests in the laboratory were used to check for cracks. Oil durability was checked by accurately weighing pieces of the rubber before and after a hot oil bath. Investigations were also made of hardness and resilience at different temperatures.

Quality-control costs were carefully monitored, Scania constantly seeking the optimum inspection/cost ratio. The

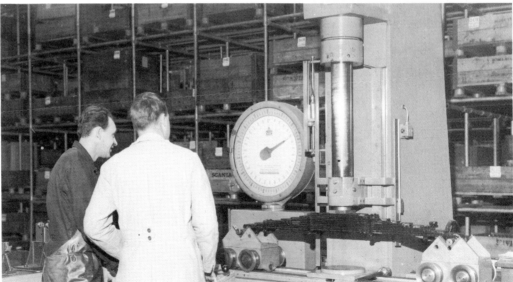

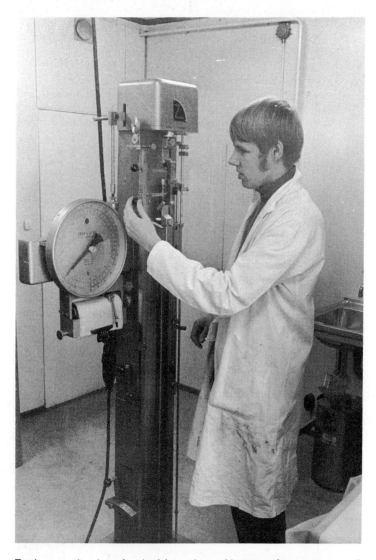

Testing a coolant hose for elasticity under a wide range of temperatures and conditions was just one of many quality tests made on components in the 1960s.

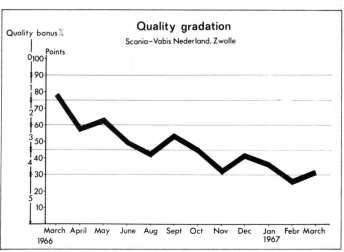

Quality gradation
Scania–Vabis Nederland, Zwolle

Quality bonus %

Points

A quality bonus scheme was operated at Scania's Zwolle factory in The Netherlands in the 1960s, workers receiving a bonus related to the quality level achieved.

management also carefully studied the psychological aspects of inspection to find out why, for example, inspectors sometimes preferred to report cheaper defects than expensive ones. The management also considered purely physical aspects, such as sharpness of vision and how these affected the quality of inspection work. They also examined such things as lighting, incomplete instructions, and so on. In inspection work, Scania had found that alertness played an important part, especially as visual checking was the dominant function. Accuracy of such work fell off rapidly, it was found; during special tests it was ascertained that accuracy in micrometer readings began to fall off after only 15 minutes' work.

Scania accordingly tried, wherever inspection work could be given over entirely to machines, to make the signalling of defects as strong as possible. Visual instruments, therefore, were often fitted with sound and light signals.

To make sure chassis leaving the works were as good as they could be, a scheme was introduced whereby examples were picked out every day for a quality audit. This involved an expert group inspecting and testing the functioning of the

These two pictures of the main Scania plant at Södertälje give a clear indication of the spaciousness of the facilities and the attractive manner in which they were laid out.

vehicle. Their observations were recorded on a special document, and any chassis defects found were graded in accordance with a special scale where smaller defects, not having a direct bearing on functioning, were rated one or five minus points. Defects that could affect operation were awarded 10 or 30 points, while those related to road safety earned 50 points.

By plotting out the points scored by the tested chassis Scania was then able to get a picture of the general quality situation. If, during this inspection, a serious defect in a vehicle was detected, the corresponding item or function was checked on all vehicles produced immediately before and after until all defective vehicles were located.

This system also formed a personal incentive. At Scania's Zwolle works, for example, the assembly line workers were given a special bonus which related to the quality level achieved, an assembly job being divided between different groups to generate continuous competition between the groups to see who could bring in the best quality bonus.

Today, this essentially is still the quality-control system,

The cab assembly line at Södertälje showing the overhead line which feeds the cabs at the appropriate point on to the chassis assembly line.

although since then it has been updated and modified to make it even more efficient. This came about through the construction of a new 2,310 m² final inspection facility for chassis at Södertälje in 1973, when a kilometre-long test track was also added to the quality-control facilities.

There is still, however, the meticulous final delivery inspection of vehicles leaving the production line. This occurs in the special building constructed in 1975 and set aside for this purpose. The vehicles are then test-driven and warmed-up on the special track, each one then being diverted into a quality-control building and submitted to the detailed quality-control schedule. By random selection, a vehicle may be pulled out for total dismantling and 100 per cent inspection,

when bolt torque adjustments and similar assembly line variables are checked.

The engine is bench-tested for many hours at varying loads and speeds, engine performance being closely monitored and its performance recorded in detail. The figures that result are then compared with design performance specifications and the engine adjusted where necessary.

Scania also recognizes that quality-control has an important part to play in the development of both its production techniques and its products. Accordingly, a system has been established for feeding information from the quality-control department back to the production line to eliminate fault conditions at source.

Apart from the spectacular development of the main chassis assembly works at Södertälje and the systems that went with it, there were other notable developments there and at outside factories. In 1967, at the Södertälje plant, for example, an up-to-date automatic hardening shop was brought into operation in the gearbox shop to increase plant capacity by 100 per cent. A further extension of 4,500 m² was made, in 1970, to the gearbox plant, in addition to the construction of a 650 m² area underground.

At Lulea, at the same time, work was in hand to complete the company's new 11,200 m² press shop to make side-members, cross-members, bumpers and rear axle housings. It must have seemed that the construction work would never end for it was not long after this shop was in full production that work started on a 3,500 m² extension and a 600 m² storage area there which, like the extension of the gearbox plant, was completed in 1970.

The company's cab-making complex, operated under the name Scania-Hylter AB at Oskarshamn, had had to be expanded to cope with the demand of the new chassis

Extreme winter conditions can be reproduced in Scania's Arctic chamber at Södertälje where the temperature can be lowered to minus 40 degrees C. But extensive testing in vehicles' natural environment also plays an important part in the company's product-proving programme.

Testing for hot weather conditions includes this performance evaluation of the air-conditioning system under the 'Sahara sun'.

Expansion is not without its problems. As a manufacturer's vehicle park increases, so does the need for replacement parts and a more elaborate system for storing and issuing them. Thus, in 1975, Scania had to increase the warehousing area of its parts department from 25,800 m² to 40,000 m² and improve the already automated parts-handling procedures.

This development reflected Scania's continuing determination not to fall behind other European manufacturers in any area of truck production. It could be seen, too, in the establishment, in 1975, of a modern 1,730 m² paint shop, which in its construction and paint application methods reflected Scania's awareness of the massive forward strides made by automotive paint manufacturers in this period, in both the product and its application.

The management was not only aware of the need to plough money into production facilities. It was acutely aware of the need to keep itself at the forefront in research and development. Accordingly, 40 million Swedish crowns were devoted to doubling the size of the company's chassis laboratory, a project which was completed in 1977. It included the construction of 10 vehicle bays, one with a chassis dynamometer, and the allocation of extra space to increase the number of test rigs. Additions were also made to the vehicle electrics laboratory and model shop.

In 1980, Scania says that production and engineering precision have been developed to such a degree with its products that the practice of classifying parts to tolerance — a common practice in many other companies — has been eliminated. This, it comments, offers significant advantages on the assembly line and obviates the enormous spare-parts inventory inherent in tolerance-classification systems. In practice, this means that there is no A-B-C grading by tolerance specifications of such parts as liners and pistons.

Reference has already been made to the high level of working conditions in Scania factories. These, the company emphasizes, are the subject of continuous study in close co-operation with the personnel employed in them. The object is to make each plant not only safer, but also a more pleasant place to work in. This study work is carried out by ergonomic design staff from the management and specialist personnel sponsored by the trade unions. A two-way flow of

assembly operation in Södertälje, so it, too, was extended by 1,400 m² in 1970, the work performed including a new below-ground-level press and assembly shop.

But expansion in 1970 did not end there. The rapidly growing production volumes had been putting pressure on engine test facilities, so a fully automated engine test centre was installed in the central laboratory. This permitted simulation of 1,000 kilometres of road work in one hour.

Things, however, moved so swiftly that even these developments were not enough, for in 1974 further expansion work was undertaken, at a cost of 12.5 million Swedish crowns, involving extensions to the diesel engine and transmission laboratories. This doubled both the performance-testing and vehicle and component life-testing capacities.

The move was made with three purposes in mind — to reduce research and development time for new engines, increase capacity for developing work on exhaust gas emission problems and vehicle noise.

Chassis shop manager Nils Nyström together with production line foremen and operatives grouped around the first T-range vehicle to be built before it left the factory in January 1980.

Working on one of the first T-range models to be built at Södertälje in January 1980 with an impressive range of component storage bins conveniently to hand.

The bonnet and mudguards of the 1980 T-range vehicles are moulded in glass-reinforced plastics. Here, a unit is being added to the chassis and cab prior to the addition of electrical equipment.

information on the production process results, and this has had a considerable spin-off in the form of product and product-engineering improvement suggestions.

In recent years, an increasing number of industrial robots has been introduced to rationalize manufacturing processes, and here a prime consideration, says Scania, has been the improvement of the working environment. Use of robot technology, it is pointed out, not only enables monotonous and back-breaking work to be handled by machines, but permits a higher degree of accuracy in quality-control and precision manufacture. This automatically reduces the risk of out-of-specification parts inadvertantly coming on to the production line.

As Scania moves into the 1980s, the company's engineering research-and-development and test facilities are amongst the best in Europe. On the production front, its Swedish plants are again amongst the most modern in Europe in terms of buildings, layout and manufacturing equipment. The base is a formidably strong one for further expansion of the Scania range in the 1980s.

Chapter 5

South American ventures

By the 1960s, Scania's overseas sales activities had become a main platform of the company's marketing programme. It was realised that Sweden and all the other Scandinavian countries put together would never generate a sufficiently large market for Scania products. To survive, let alone grow, it was necessary to look further afield.

Up to this point, the most important single overseas operation was, of course, that in Brazil, which by now was firmly established. Originally (from 1953) a company called Vemag had built and marketed Scanias from ckd sets imported from Södertälje. Scania diesel-engine construction began in Brazil with the same company in 1959, but by 1970 it had become apparent that chassis assembly, sales and service would have to be taken over from Vemag. As a result, a completely new manufacturing plant was built by Scania at Sao Bernardo, 20 kilometres from Sao Paulo, and was opened in 1962. But there were difficult times ahead. Brazil was in the midst of a period of galloping inflation, and a fairly deep economic depression hit that country. Scania-Vabis do Brasil, fresh from heavy investment in a new plant, suffered as a result and had an uneasy period financially at this time. However, its situation improved, and in 1964 a total of 731 trucks and buses and 150 marine and industrial engines were produced.

It remained a very uncertain period economically in Brazil's history, nevertheless, for inflation, running at 60 to 70 per cent a year at this time, had not yet peaked. It was to do so in 1965 — at 90.8 per cent — before it started to drop.

It was the uncertainty over economic conditions that, perhaps, led Scania's Brazilian company to peg along at much the same rate of production throughout the 1960s, although it was to receive a boost as the 1970s dawned. In 1968, production totalled 710 vehicles, a figure which moved to 782 in 1969, 863 in 1970 and 887 in 1971 before bursting through the four-figure barrier in a big way in 1972 to reach a total of 1,327. This put Scania firmly into the leading position in the heaviest class of vehicle in Brazil (30 to 40 tons gross weight) and the company's reputation was number-one as well.

Not surprisingly, Brazil was at this time totally a bonneted-vehicle market for Scania, reflecting perhaps the American truck industry's influence, which is strong in South America, and perhaps, too, the similar long-distance haulage conditions that prevail both in Brazil and in the USA. Also, of course, bonneted models were a Scania speciality anyway. Scania kept very much to one model, its 111 series, in this period — a robust design which could, and did, stand up to a great deal of abuse.

It is interesting to relate Scania's sales performance improvement in the late-1960s and early-1970s to economic and social conditions in Brazil, for they are strongly and closely related. Brazil ranks as the world's fifth largest country — after the Soviet Union, Canada, China and the USA — with a surface area of 8 million sq km. This alone makes it significant from the transport viewpoint. Add the

Two aerial views of the Scania plant situated at Sao Bernardo do Campo, some 20 kilometres from the centre of Sao Paulo, as it was in 1970, above, and nine years later, on the right.

A late-1970s photograph of a five-axled Brazilian-built Scania 110 hauling a gas tank semi-trailer.

fact that the country's 100 million population is largely concentrated within a strip 300 kilometres wide in the industrial South East region, which includes the cities of Sao Paulo, Belo Horizonte and Rio de Janeiro, and in addition to Rio the ports of Vitoria and Santos, and it is immediately apparent that there is a population imbalance. This is a situation which the Brazilian Government recognized some years ago and has been striving to correct with massive industrial relocation projects and location incentives for companies setting up industrial activities.

Add to this situation an equally massive road-building programme to link the new industrial centres with the old and open-up the interior, and it becomes evident that Brazil in this period of the 1960s and 1970s has been — and still is — a truck maker's paradise. With a very limited rail system, the whole national transport policy is directed towards roads and road transport.

Road development in the period from 1965 — the date from which Brazil's current industrial development plan operated — has been little short of fantastic. In that year

there were some 12,589 kilometres of federally controlled highways and 13,835 kilometres in the state system. The 10 year plan — which was, in the event, achieved — envisaged 71,000 kilometres of paved roads in the federal and state system by 1974.

The overall plan was a box network of highways in the Pan-South American road system designed to link every country, with perhaps the most spectacular part being the Transamazonian highway to link the existing road networks serving ports in North East Brazil with the interior, right to the Peruvian Border. Such was the exciting backcloth for Scania's Brazilian truck-building operations. Demand for vehicles had to come.

By the 1970s, of course, Scania Vabis do Brasil had become SAAB-Scania do Brasil S.A. (the name changed in 1970) and under this title production moved up steadily, 1978 seeing 3,500 trucks and buses built for the first time. A similar figure was achieved in 1979.

It should be pointed out that almost the entire production process from component manufacture to finished products

The Scania production line at Tucuman, in The Argentine. This plant, in north-western Argentina and operated by SAAB-Scania Argentina SA, has around 800 employees.

Fitting suspension units at the Scania plant in Brazil in 1972.

for sale to leading makers of construction and industrial plant and equipment.

There is now an unusual activity centred on Scania's Brazilian plant. It is a focal point for the development of heavy vehicles powered by engines run on alcohol fuels. One of Brazil's most important products is sugar cane. As Brazil at the moment has no crude oil the Government is limiting oil imports and has introduced legislation to encourage the use of vegetable-based alcohol fuels; ethanol.

This programme is so far advanced that the Government's three-year plan, starting January 1, 1980, envisages a production of 900,000 alcohol-powered vehicles in the plan period, with 250,000 in 1980, 300,000 in 1981 and 350,000 in 1983. There is also a three-year programme on adaptations, which envisages 80,000 conversions in 1980, 90,000 in 1981 and 100,000 in 1982. The scale of the exercise is revealed by figures issued by the Brazilian Association of Automotive Manufacturers (ANFAVEA), which has indicated that

takes place in Brazil. This is a situation which has come about by necessity. Brazil's policy has been to encourage the development of its own industries and has offered extensive incentives to companies prepared to set-up in development areas and manufacture virtually 100 per cent domestically. With the carrot there is also the whip in the form of swingeing taxes on imported components.

Since its construction in 1962, Scania's Sao Bernardo plant has tripled in size and now occupies a land area of 240,000 m² and a factory floor area of 85,000 m². This expansion occurred in the mid-1970s and concurrently there was an expansion of the model range to the point where six basic truck models and three buses are produced. The trucks are the L111, LS111 and LT111 bonneted models and the LK141, LKS141 and LKT141 forward-control designs. The buses are the B111, BR116 and the B111 articulated bus. In addition to the vehicles, the loose engine side has steadily developed so that today the D11, the DS11, the D14 and the DS14 are built

A late-1970s photograph of the Brazilian factory's production line in the most recently built part of the plant.

A typical Brazilian-built Scania, circa 1970, pictured hauling a tank semi-trailer on the road to Santos.

An L71 artic from the 1950s operating as a cattle transporter in The Argentine.

Brazil's plan is to produce 10.7 million gallons of alcohol fuels annually by 1985.

Obviously this programme will have its biggest impact on private cars — for which already it is possible to get alcohol fuel from the pump at filling stations — but there is an equal impact on commercial vehicles, where not only Scania but other leading manufacturers like Daimler-Benz are involved. Scania's initial efforts have been directed at engines which

Durability-testing a special-purpose 110 Super three-axled tractor unit with Scania's Sao Paulo plant in the background.

L64 truck chassis delivered in 1952 formed the basis of these Brazilian buses, the bodywork of which was constructed locally.

obviously is more economic to run one large vehicle than several small ones.

With a firm base in the South American continent, it was a logical step to look at other countries in that region to secure and expand markets. Up to 1966 Scania had sold 500 vehicles in Peru, and when the opportunity arose to acquire the shares of Diesel Motors S.A. of Lima — then the Scania general agent in that country — the company took it. The facility was not a particularly large one but, employing some 100 people, it did have an assembly plant, service workshops and spare parts stocks, although today it is essentially regarded as a marketing company as opposed to a manufacturing facility.

A more significant move came in the 1970s when Scania decided to build a factory in Tucuman, in The Argentine. This 30,000 m² plant came on stream in 1976, building L111 trucks and BR116 bus chassis and having a planned production capacity of 1,500 heavy vehicles a year. It was also designed as a gearbox manufacturing facility and, in fact, gearboxes built there are exported to Brazil, where they are installed in Sao Bernardo-built vehicles. The plant also exports transmission components to The Netherlands and Sweden.

The Tucuman plant does not make all components used in the vehicle's construction, although they represent a high percentage. There is no cab-making facility, for example, so cabs are imported in knocked-down form from Sweden, as are rear-axle casings and gearbox components. Scania started laying plans for this facility towards the end of the 1960s. The company points out that The Argentine had long been an important export market for Scania trucks, and Scania had a general agent who imported the vehicles.

Rigorous import restrictions faced overseas truck manufacturers, however, and most of them abandoned the market. This nearly happened with Scania. It so happened, however, that the Argentinian Government, which was faced with retrenchment of its sugar industry in the Tucuman region, decided to try to attract new industries to the region. Saab-Scania expressed interest in building a truck plant and in 1972 successfully tendered and were given permission to go ahead with this venture. The Tucuman plant employs 800 people.

run on a mixture of conventional diesel and ethanol, but the long-term plan is to run 'diesels' on pure alcohol.

Exports from Sao Bernardo currently represent 25 per cent of total sales, the main markets being in other South American countries and Africa. In addition, parts and components are being exported to Sweden, The Netherlands, The Argentine and Australia.

Today, there are close on 40,000 Scania vehicles on Brazilian roads and its share of the Brazilian heavy truck (30 to 40 tons) market is 38 per cent. It should be pointed out, however, that this is a relatively small sector of the truck market numerically; it accounts for just 8 per cent of the 800,000 truck park in Brazil. Scania says, however, that prospects are bright because, with the energy crisis, it

Versatility! This 1960s Scania tractor unit, right, modified for use as a recovery vehicle, endeavours to lift a crashed artic on the road between Sao Paulo and Rio de Janeiro, while another fully laden artic, below, helps with a tow line.

Above left, rough treatment for a Scania L51 seen operating in Paraguay in the 1950s. Above, barrels of wine form the payload of this L71 operating in Brazil in the late-1950s. Below left, Peru was the location of this L64 road train operating out of Lima Chiclayo with a payload of 22 tons. Below, Scania's first truck for a customer in Uruguay was this L61, which was delivered in 1951.

Chapter 6

The drive into Europe and the UK

Obviously, in retrospect, Scania made exactly the right choice in choosing Brazil for its first overseas manufacturing centre. Was the management foresighted or just plain lucky? The former, one suspects, judging from the company's selection of its other choices for overseas activities; its move into mainland Europe was a case in point.

Since Sweden was not a member of the European Economic Community, to get into the Community countries effectively meant setting-up a manufacturing facility within the EEC.

Zwolle, in The Netherlands, was chosen, and in 1963 Scania Nederland BV was formed. The assembly plant established there, covering a total area of 27,000 m², came on stream towards the end of 1964, producing some 200 chassis in its first year. Scania has a second plant in The Netherlands, at Meppel, which is quite near Zwolle. This was acquired in 1966 when the company bought the Swedish bodybuilding firm of Be-Ge Karosserifabrik, of Oskarshamn. Its Meppel plant was converted to producing Scania cabs, which until then had been imported from Sweden.

The Dutch factories today are responsible for the assembly and marketing of Scania trucks and diesel engines in The Netherlands, Belgium, Luxembourg, France, Germany and Italy — all of the original EEC countries, in fact. The success of the operation can be measured by the fact that current production is 4,500 chassis annually, along with some 300 engines. Not that this all stems from the plant as it was in 1964. In 1973 the main assembly hall of the factory in Zwolle was expanded by 4,380 m² to give a total area of 23,000 m², a completely new quality-control centre was installed, and a new test track built. At Meppel, the cab production facility was totally modernized and re-equipped.

Scania Nederland currently assembles Scania's complete truck range, but the main components, including engines, transmissions, propeller-shafts and rear axles, are designed, developed and manufactured in Sweden. Other components, such as tyres and fuel injection pumps, are purchased from manufacturers in EEC countries and supplied direct to the Dutch factories.

Marketing and distribution is handled in the older-established Scania territories. The Netherlands in a strong market for Scania, for example, and here Beers' Zonen NV is responsible for marketing, and has been since the first truck was shipped to Holland in 1946.

The second oldest relationship is with the importer for Belgium and Luxembourg, Denonville SA, which has been doing the job since 1949. Relatively recently — in February 1979 — Scania acquired Denonville, with its 350 employees, its Brussels headquarters and its sales and service outlets.

Scania's organizations in the other EEC countries are, however, more recent, and a different marketing formula has been pursued in Germany and France, where Scania Deutschland GmbH has handled imports since its formation in 1970. Later still, in 1976, Scania France SA was formed,

A view of the Zwolle assembly line, on a factory site 100 km east of Amsterdam, where the full range of Scania medium-heavy and heavy trucks are produced.

and a 7,000 m² facility built to house offices, equipment, workshop and spare parts. This company took over the Scania market franchise from Société Industrielle Automobile SA, distributors for Scania vehicles since 1961. This leaves Italy, a country to which the Zwolle plant has been exporting since 1974, when Italscandia Autocarri SpA of Trento was awarded the Scania franchise.

As for the size of the market in these countries, The Netherlands leads with some 17,500 vehicles sold to date, then Belgium and Luxembourg with 12,000, France with 8,000, West Germany with 7,500 and Italy 2,000. In both France and West Germany Scania is the market leader amongst the heavy-vehicle importers.

The range offered by Scania from Zwolle extends from the 16.5 tons gross vehicle weight L81, powered by a 163 bhp

(DIN) engine, to the Scania LT146 which, with the Scania V8 engine developing 375 bhp (DIN), is designed for operation at gross weights of anything up to 70 tons or more.

Although Scania appreciated the necessity of establishing a manufacturing base in the EEC territories in the early days of the Common Market, the same necessity was not present in the European Free Trade Area, of which Sweden was a member.

In the early-1960s, Britain had one of the strongest home markets for trucks in the world, let alone Europe. The numbers of imported goods vehicles, particularly heavies, could almost be counted on the fingers of one hand. Daimler-Benz was one of the few makers to have tried to get established, but with a singular lack of success. Most overseas manufacturers backed-off from the tough UK home market, but this was a situation that was to alter dramatically as the face of European transport changed.

The first feature which contributed to this was the motorway-building boom of the 1950s and 1960s, which created a European motorway network. This stimulated a

The Scania Nederland BV factory at Zwolle, which came on stream in 1964 and where 800 people are employed to produce 4,500 vehicles annually.

Operating with a drawbar trailer, this LB81, registered in 1979, is fitted with the Scania 8-litre naturally aspirated diesel engine.

need for maximum-capacity motorway-hauling rigs running at gross weights dictated by those countries which had the highest legal weight limits in Europe — countries like The Netherlands, Belgium, France and Germany, where 38 tons and more was the norm. International transport of goods by road was facilitated by the appearance of the TIR (Transport International Routiers) Customs Convention, which permitted the movement of vehicles of an approved construction under customs seal across frontiers throughout Europe.

Then, too, there was the rapid development of roll-on, roll-off ferry services between Britain and Europe, and later between the countries surrounding the Baltic and, later still, the Mediterranean. A final factor, which was to change the face of transport in Europe, was the 'container revolution', as it has come to be known. Shipping companies, moving away from conventional cargo carriers, started to construct ships purpose-built for container carrying, with containers made to the standards of the International Standards Organization

A 1980s Scania LB81 hauling a Taskers Trailers curtain-sided semi-trailer. The towing bracket discreetly recessed into the front bumper is a useful feature of the design.

As far back as 1953, when this photograph was taken, Scanias were recognized as international haulage vehicles. This L60 operated between Amsterdam and Rome.

Direct export was the rule in the early-1950s, when this batch of Scanias was pictured being loaded for delivery to Turkey.

Some of the first Scania vehicles to operate in Britain were these LB76 articulated outfits put on the road in 1967 by Jameson, above, J & H Transport Services, above right, and British Ropes, right.

(ISO) in modules of 10ft, 20ft and 40ft long. To carry them to and from the ports purpose-built heavy goods vehicles were required.

Britain was slow to react to meet this situation. For years the eight-wheeled rigid vehicle operating at 24 tons gross with a deck length of 30ft had virtually been the largest vehicle on the roads. The biggest articulated outfit could operate at up to 28 tons gross. Neither type of vehicle was economically suited to the needs of the new era in European transport. The legislators lagged, and it was not until 1964 that Britain changed its construction requirements to permit the operation of bigger, heavier machines.

Even then it was a case of too little, too late to meet the challenge of both European vehicle manufacturers and European hauliers, for the maximum weight limit went up to 32 tons and not the 38 tons level which would have made the British product and service competitive. The British vehicle manufacturers had a long way to go to catch up and it was to take them 10 years and more to produce a product range to compare with those offered by manufacturers on the European mainland.

Scania was the first manufacturer in Europe fully to realise the marketing opportunity which had appeared in the UK, which was also a member of EFTA, and in 1964 the Swedish company established Scania Vabis Great Britain Ltd, with head offices in London.

Scania's marketing philosophy when the Swedish company was launched on the British market was explained by C.J. Lewenhagen, Vice-President of Scania-Vabis, at a press conference in London on August 22, 1966. This is what he had to say: 'It is not only trucks, buses and engines which we sell. We also try to sell untroubled economic transportation. We offer a well-developed service and spare parts organization in many of the countries in Europe, and we are very anxious to be able to put workshops at our customers' disposal which are equipped with qualified personnel, accurate special tools and spare parts supplied without delay.

'Why is that of particular interest to British customers? Not

More than just a heavy lorry, this Scania LBS141 six-wheeler, built in 1978 and seen hauling an Italian-built Rolfo drawbar trailer, is also equipped for carrying demountable bodies. The air suspension is pumped up to permit the bodies to be raised, then the legs of the bodies can be swung down. Deflation of the air bags leaves the bodies standing for the chassis to be driven away. The outfit is run by a Milan haulier between Italy and Germany.

A 1979 LB111 tractor unit hauling a Crane Fruehauf insulated semi-trailer fitted with Thermo-King refrigeration equipment.

only because of the growing number of hauliers who work on international trade routes operating with freights all over Europe, but also for transport agents who co-operate with hauliers domiciled in, for example, The Netherlands.

'We intend to offer the British customers all that we have been able to offer customers in other countries, where we have made ourselves well-known. We consider Great Britain to be a large missing cog in our export organization, which we are now trying to fit in. We can manage it, however, as we now have the trucks that suit your market, namely trucks with cab-over-engine and right-hand drive. The adjustment of the British gross weight regulations has given us an opportunity to satisfy a demand for our products.'

He was at pains to convince his audience that the Swedish challenge would not hit the British industry. How wrong he

was! This is what he said: 'Our efforts to introduce ourselves on the British market may seem to some of you to be a potential threat to your export-import balance which, as we are fully aware, is one of the most anxious problems for your Government to solve. However, our export to Britain of a couple of hundred units represents only a splash in the ocean. The import of vehicles, regardless of type, to Sweden from Great Britain in 1965 amounted to £15,000,000; the corresponding Swedish export during the same period amounted to £2,500,000.

'Our company imported British products, such as brake equipment, fuel injections and forgings during 1965 to a value of £4,000,000 which is more than 50 per cent more than the total Swedish export of vehicles to Great Britain. To balance this import we would have to multiply our own export several

A Dutch Scania LB76 hauling a container-carrying semi-trailer alongside the docks at Rotterdam.

This Italian-registered Scania 111 is designed for intensive duties in both short-haul and long-distance transport. The engine options on this model are the turbocharged DS11-01, developing 280 bhp, or the DS11-02 power unit, which develops 305 bhp.

One of the most popular models in Britain in the 1970s was the Scania 110 Super, basically a turbocharged-engined model in the LB111 series. This 1972 vehicle of Southern British Road Services is seen competing with a Seddon in the finals of the 1975 Lorry Driver of the Year.

times over.'

As a kind of footnote it is appropriate to point out that the 1980 level of UK sales at 1,500 trucks costing say, on average, £25,000 each to the haulier, adds up to £37.5m without bus and component sales.

It was not until the end of 1966 that Scania vehicles started to roll into Britain. This coincided with the abolition of tariffs between the EFTA countries in 1967. It explains the decision to set up a marketing company in Britain rather than a manufacturing subsidiary. Not that the situation was totally rosy, as Gosta Nilsson, managing director of Scania, was at pains to point out in an address in Stockholm towards the end of 1966. He said: 'Within the EFTA the final abolition of tariffs takes place on January 1, 1967, except in the case of Finland, which reaches the zero level one year later. This will naturally entail quite a number of advantages, but the situation is not so uniformly bright as one might be led to believe.'

He went on to say: 'The discrimination arising through the

EEC co-operation will obviously exert its full effect. On the other hand the advantages which membership of the EFTA ought to confer will be curtailed, which will be due in some extent to protectionistic measures of some of the EFTA countries. Norway, for example, to judge by all the signs, will retain a so-called fiscal tariff of 20 per cent and Portugal a similar tariff of 8.8 escudos per kilo.

'An important prerequisite of the ability to compete is naturally the possession of a proper type programme. There is an insistent demand for versatility, which will surely increase as the number of special body constructions grows. It is necessary to go along with this trend, but at the same time, of course, one has to be wary of frittering away one's resources. If one looks at Scania-Vabis' type programme for 1950 and compared it with that of today, one may be tempted to believe that we have abandoned our previously restrained line, but this is not the case. The fact of the matter is that important basic components are utilized in various combinations in our programme, which keeps down the numbers of parts.

UK bulk haulier Sayers Transport Services put this handsome LB111 on the road in 1979. It is fitted with numerous cab extras including an external sun vizor and two-tone continental-type horns.

'Swedish truck manufacture has a rational programme which in very satisfactory fashions meets the needs of the market without being unduly fragmented. Many of our competitors have an even more multi-faceted programme, which must, however, create problems not only in research and production, but also in the distribution stage in respect of spare-part supplies, workshop service and sales activities.'

He gave an indication of what he thought about the future. 'I believe,' he said, 'that not least among the reasons for our own success is the fact that we have concentrated our energies on our speciality, and I believe that it is of the greatest importance to abide by this policy.'

The vehicle chosen for the British market was the LB76, converted to right-hand drive and with a shorter-than-normal wheelbase. Features of this vehicle, like the spring parking brake and three-line air brakes, were something of a novelty to British operators.

Success was immediate, especially amongst the international hauliers running into Europe. Higher engine power than the levels to which they were used, plus good ride and handling characteristics and a comfortable cab, led the LB76 to become equally popular amongst operators and drivers alike.

The Scania vehicle park in Britain built up quickly and very soon Scania was exporting over 1,000 vehicles annually to the UK. In 1980 new registrations were expected to be around the same figure as the previous year — 1,500.

Scania's overseas expansion efforts in South America,

Registered in 1978, this Scania LB111 is seen hauling a load of ice cream for the well-known Wall's company.

This Scania 16-tons gvw LB81 can accommodate both short and long Macklift skips of up to 22 cubic yards capacity and can lift a weight of 9.5 tons. The vehicle has a wheelbase of 4.2 metres and is equipped with a naturally aspirated 8-litre Scania six-cylinder diesel engine and five-speed all-synchromesh gearbox.

One of the first Scania L80 models assembled in Iraq, this vehicle was equipped with a dumper body for construction work.

Europe and the UK have perhaps overshadowed developments elsewhere. There are a surprisingly large number of these, notably in Africa, the Middle East and Australia. Scania's bonneted models have a particular appeal in African and Middle-East territories. In fact, today, a high proportion of the total production of Scania bonneted vehicles finds its way to countries in these regions.

They are assembled in a number of countries as a result. Morocco was one of the first. Back in 1969 the Moroccan authorities granted Scania permission for the assembly and limited manufacture of both trucks and buses at a plant to be built in Casablanca. The company formed to handle this was Scania Maghreb S.A., which never really got going because of Moroccan independence and restrictions which were imposed on development by overseas companies.

In 1979 Scania announced the conclusion of an agreement with the Moroccan company Cogespar SA, to form a joint company, Scania Maroc SA, to assemble and market Scania trucks and buses in Morocco. It was stated then that the new assembly plant was to be built on the outskirts of Casablanca and would become operational in the autumn of 1980. The initial production plan is for the assembly of 300 to 400 trucks and buses a year.

The agreement indicated that assembly kits for the Moroccan factory would be supplied by Scania factories in Sweden. A number of components, including springs, tyres and batteries would be manufactured locally, and the new company would employ about 100 factory workers and 40 office staff.

Morocco has enforced a total restriction on imports of fully assembled trucks and buses since the beginning of the 1960s, and the establishment of a domestic assembly plant is a prior condition of marketing commercial vehicles and buses in the country. Since this announcement, however, the development has run into problems and the project, at best, is delayed.

Dar-es-Salaam, in Tanzania, was to be the next African location for Scania to provide sales-and-service back-up for Scania vehicles and owners following the successful sale of several hundred vehicles to this developing country. This gave Scania a strong base in Tanzania and the company's reputation there grew. As a result of this, pilot assembly projects were embarked upon and early in 1977 the Swedish

Scania L110 general haulage vehicles arrive at a cement plant in Iraq to pick up a load.

company and the National Development Corporation in Tanzania started formal discussions about building a truck-assembly plant.

These reached fruition in 1978 when an agreement was concluded with Tanzania's NDC to establish a new company called the Tanzania Automobile Manufacturing Company (TAMCO), to be located at Kibaha (35 kilometres outside Dar-es-Salaam), to build Scania's LB81 model and a number of bus chassis, with an annual production capacity of 1,200 chassis. This factory was due to come on stream in 1980.

In 1971 Scania and the Ministry of Industry in Iraq got together to conclude a somewhat similar agreement to the Moroccan one for the assembly of Scania trucks and buses in that country. This was a success right from the start, partly perhaps because Scania had been selling trucks to that country since 1958. It was agreed that a plant would be built close to Baghdad and that Scania should supply ckd assembly kits for both truck and bus chassis.

This was where Scania's responsibility ended, however, as it was agreed that the Iraq Government should be responsible for the assembly and sales of vehicles in that country. This has been a successful venture and the Baghdad plant has built an increasing number of vehicles annually, mainly L111 and LT111 series, since 1972, when the plant came on stream. By 1978 a total of 5,000 vehicles had been built there and 1979 was to see an out-and-out record of 3,250 vehicles built, 2,150 of the 110 series and 870 buses, all BF111s.

Scania obtained a presence in Australia in the same year as the Iraq development — 1972. There, SAAB-Scania Australia Pty Ltd was formed to market Scania products, and work was

Workers at the Baghdad plant celebrating the construction of their 100th Scania vehicle.

were assembled there for the Australian market in 1979. Scania is, however, expanding fast in Australia, and apart from having increased the size of existing branches and opened new depots in 1979, the Australian company in April opened the new computerized national parts warehouse at Somerton.

started on a 1,500 m² truck and bus sales and service facility in Melbourne, which was completed in 1973. There was a similar development at Moorbank, Sydney.

The potential of the Australian market was extensive, however, and the decision was taken to start assembling vehicles. In May, 1979, assembly started at Campbellfield, Melbourne, yet development was such that, within two years, it was found necessary to move to bigger premises at Somerton offering 3,000 m² of factory space and a further 1,300 m² of storage and warehouse facilities.

A measure of the size of the operation is that 273 Scanias

Syria is a market in which operators love to decorate their vehicles with protective grilles, like this example seen on an L7150 in 1956.

A strong show of interest in two L81s from a camel in Syria, the tanker displaying one of the fashionable extra grilles.

Angola has long been a good market for Scania. Here is an L51 fording a swollen river there in 1960.

A Scania L51 pictured in Morocco in 1957. By the signwriting on the front bumper it looks as though the driver might treat the vehicle like a home, although it probably means that he spends most of his time travelling between Casablanca and Marrakesh!

Chapter 7

The environmental contribution

Scania's acute awareness of the need to maintain the highest possible levels of working conditions in the company's plants has been matched by its environmental studies on commercial vehicles and their operation.

There is no doubt that the immense improvement in commercial vehicle cab design in Europe in the 1960s and 1970s, for example, began in Scandinavia. Improved safety was obviously the main reason for Sweden adopting its cab strength test (see Chapter 2), once again not unassociated with its timber industry, where a falling tree trunk could do an awful lot of damage to someone in a flimsily built vehicle.

However, Scania has always taken steps beyond what has been legally needed, insisting on cabs offering a good working environment, providing generous all-round vision from the driver's seat, which itself had to be comfortable and fully adjustable to suit the height and weight of the driver. On the Scania philosophy instruments were required to be easy to see and controls ready to hand. Moreover, for a cab to be comfortable it had to be well insulated against noise, heat and cold, but well heated and ventilated. These things are taken for granted today, but manufacturers considered them very little in the 1950s when Scania first really started paying attention to these features.

Scania also realised early on that a driver needed a lot of muscle to handle a heavily laden vehicle without power-assisted steering (see also Chapter 2). As a consequence the company was one of the pioneers — in 1954 — of power-steering fitment on heavies to ease the driver's job and make the vehicles safer.

On general safety, Scania has been involved in all the work conducted by the very safety-conscious Swedish Government. In Sweden, use of headlamps in daylight — on trucks as well as cars — is the norm, and in fact is prescribed in the Swedish Highway Code. Moreover, headlamp washers and wipers have been standard on all motor vehicles in Sweden since January 1, 1973.

Another mandatory requirement, but in this case affecting goods vehicles only, concerns bumpers and under-ride guards. Designed primarily, of course, to reduce the danger to other road-users in the event of a collision, under-ride guards also became obligatory on all heavy trucks and trailers manufactured after January 1, 1973, and had to conform to certain standards drawn up by the Swedish Road Safety Board.

A great deal of work was done in the 1970s on fenders to protect pedestrians and cyclists. These consist of guards running along the side of the vehicle and lightly tensioned protective wires between truck and trailer.

Probably the most significant area to which Scania has contributed environmentally is, however, in the direction of noise control — not just in-cab but on-highway noise which goes beyond the minimum requirements currently laid down by international bodies. The European Economic Community, for example, laid down maximum noise levels in the early-1970s which came into operation at the start of April 1980. These maximum limits were, however, already in existence in the domestic legislation of individual countries before that date. It is worth noting the levels of noise which manufacturers had to meet. Using the International Standards Organization (ISO) method of testing, the following EEC commercial vehicle limits applied:

Trucks up to 3.5 tons gross weight   81 dB(A)

Trucks over 3.5 tons tons gross weight   86 dB(A)

Trucks of 12 tons gvw and more and with engine
power exceeding 200 bhp (DIN)   88 dB(A)

For tolerances on the instruments 1 dB(A) is added to these figures.

There are also limits for buses and much of Scania's noise-control work has been concerned with this type of vehicle, and its success in this area has been such that by the beginning of the 1970s it had reduced noise levels from 85-87 dB(A) to approximately 77 dB(A) according to ISO standards.

It is basically true, of course, that the more powerful the

Headlamp wipers like this have been a legal requirement in Sweden since January 1, 1973.

Built at Scania's Zwolle plant in The Netherlands, this LB86 model is equipped with Nooteboom's container-handling system and an Atlas hydraulically operated loading crane.

Comparative performance testing of Scania products is aided by in-service comparisons between vehicles with the active help of the Swedish haulage co-operatives. This photograph shows two Scania 141s being operated by AB Svenska Godcentraler (ASG) and Bilspedition.

engine fitted, the noisier it will be, partly due to the engine itself and partly to the operation of the larger fan needed to cool it. As a point of interest, in the work done by Scania in the early-1970s, the cooling fan fitted was found to contribute 81 dB(A). This was the last ingredient in a total noise mix of 86.5 dB(A). Tyres at 74 dB(A) and combustion and mechanical component noise of 84 dB(A) produced a total of 85 dB(A). Then induction noise through the engine sucking in air for combustion producing 77 dB(A) added a further ½ dB(A) to bring the total to 85.5 dB(A) before counting the fan noise.

The work done on the buses has since been used extensively and wherever practical on Scania's goods-vehicle models. Here are some of the points established: First, turbocharging can compensate for the increased noise generated by fitting a higher-output engine. In fact the more powerful

turbocharged engine fitted in the Scania bus noise study in place of a naturally-aspirated unit cut the noise level by 3 decibels.

Insulation of the engine compartment with fire-tested, foam plastic, noise-absorbant materials can reduce engine noise substantially. However, this, plus a higher-output engine, can give rise to cooling problems. Accordingly, a bigger fan will be necessary, but any increase in noise which might result can be checked by the fitment of a thermostatically-controlled low-rev cooling with maximized revolution rate. A special ventilating fan may also be necessary to remove hot air from an enclosed engine compartment.

Exhaust noise can be reduced to negligible levels by fitting long-life, double-resonance-chamber silencers. Special silencers fitted to outlet valves on air-brake systems eliminate

Scania's encouragement in the 1960s to manufacturers of demountable body systems is reflected in these vehicles. Above is the Hydraulex system, which pulled the body on and off the chassis using a central chain conveyor; above right is the BESIMA side loader for 20ft and 40ft ISO containers; and below is a similar system in use with bucket loaders, which were widely used in Sweden with drawbar trailers.

all noise occurring when compressed air is released from the brakes. The result of this research and development work is a relatively quiet range of heavy goods vehicles, as well as buses.

Scania was equally active in the 1960s and 1970s in trying to educate the public about diesel exhaust emissions. There was at that time considerable public concern about the effect of 'black smoke' from diesels. Scania played its part in killing canards about diesel engines and their emissions. Obviously, as a diesel engine manufacturer, it was concerned about the impression that diesel exhaust fumes were injurious. One of the points the company drew attention to was that diesels were, in fact, far less harmful than petrol engines.

The company pointed out that a diesel engine emits about 20 kg of carbon monoxide against about 350 kg for a petrol engine at a combustion of 1,000 litres of fuel. Then, warming to its turbocharged engine theme, it stressed that the amount of carbon monoxide was further reduced with a diesel engine if it was provided with turbocharging. The reason for the low content of carbon monoxide in the case of diesel engines, Scania explained, was because combustion was more complete, the diesel engine emitting instead larger quantities of carbon dioxide, which is, of course, quite harmless. With

Easy-to-hand instruments and controls are regarded by Scania as an essential aid for drivers, while the central location of the radio means that it can be operated conveniently by either occupant of the cab.

diesel fuel was (as is) lead-free. Both engine types emitted solid carbon particles, it was pointed out, and soot in small amounts (1-2 kg per 1000 litres of fuel) was produced. Through development work on the turbocharged diesel engine, however, Scania had reduced the amount of soot emitted by 90 per cent over the 10-year period to 1972.

Strangely, perhaps, from the environmental viewpoint, Scania considered that the characteristic diesel smell was that which was the most troublesome. These odourants existed in exhaust gases in quantities that were hardly measurable, it was pointed out but were, despite that, very penetrating. Scania investigated exhaust pollution extensively in the late-1960s and early-1970s to meet the then projected Swedish, British and EEC legal requirements.

The company came up with a number of targets which Tore Tysk, the head of Scania's diesel engine laboratory, set out in a paper on diesel exhaust pollution early in 1972. Looking at power required for truck and trailer combinations of 30 - 40 tons and recognizing that EEC guidelines envisaged outputs between 200 and 300 hp but that engines developing 400 bhp would probably be needed, these were the parameters: Good

turbocharging, it was stressed, the cylinders were supplied with excess air but, at the same time, burnt larger quantities of fuel to increase power and make combustion more complete. Even in dense city traffic, however, carbon monoxide only offered a marginal risk and dispersed quickly. In Stockholm, measurements made revealed that the carbon monoxide quantities (exhaust gas percentages) decreased to 25-30 per cent of the maximum value at a distance of 70 metres from the maximum value-measuring point.

Otherwise, Scania pointed out, differences between the mixture of exhaust gases with diesel and petrol engines was not all that great. The diesel engine emitted a slightly larger quantity of sulphur and nitrogen compounds than the petrol engine. But at the time Scania was emphasizing this, petrol exhaust gases contained lead, which diesel engines did not as

This two-spoke steering wheel has been designed carefully to offer maximum visibility of the instruments and control panel.

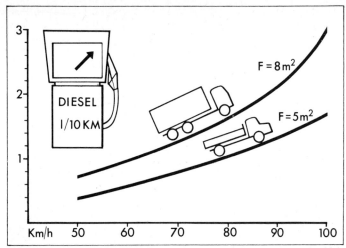

This diagram shows the higher fuel consumption of a forward-control vehicle with a high frontal area compared with a low-profile bonneted unit as the speed increases.

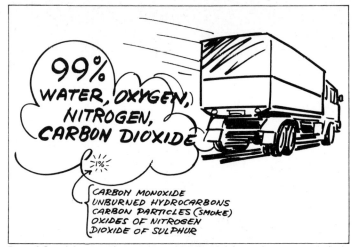

Part of Scania's campaign to show that diesel exhaust fumes are relatively harmless resulted in this sketch revealing the chemical content of diesel exhaust smoke.

economy — high engine efficiency and reliability; high degree of flexibility — the power unit should make the vehicle capable of blending in with other traffic on the roads as smoothly as possible, give good acceleration and be easy to control; low noise level — engines should make as little noise as possible and conform to legislation; and a very limited exhaust emission — they should discharge as low a volume of injurious exhaust gases as possible conforming to legislative requirements.

Measures he suggested for reducing nitrogen oxides in diesel engines included retarding the injection timing, modifying the combustion chamber, altering the compression ratio, turbocharging with intermediate cooling, recirculation of the exhaust gases and water injection. It is worth noting that all these features were subsequently given attention and the characteristics were embodied in modifications to the complete range of Scania engines.

The same applied to the measures he advocated for reducing smoke emissions. Tore Tysk suggested increasing the rate of injection, turbocharging, modifying air circulation and mixing fuel with the induction air. Some features, like turbocharging were, of course, already in use, but impact of these measures can be seen on modern roads where 'smokers' are the exception rather than the rule, as they were in the 1950s.

The most recent area of environmental research and development work tackled by Scania has been that of fuel economy. In 1977 a campaign was launched in close co-operation with Swedish haulage companies and driver trade unions. Its purpose was to reduce the overall fuel consumption of vehicles and to encourage truck drivers to adopt steadier even-speed driving techniques. Maintenance of steady speeds avoided the strains and stresses imposed on drivers by constant fluctuations and improved road safety levels.

To test this theory Scania placed three complete rigs at the disposal of transport organizations. The trucks were fitted with a fuel consumption meter, tachometer, revolution counter, tyre pressure indicator and load indicator. Values recorded on these instruments were entered by the driver in a special log book, together with time and place of departure and arrival and odometer readings.

The resultant data was computer processed and presented in tabular and graphic form. Typical information available included fuel consumption per payload ton/kilometre, engine revolutions per kilometre, running time in top gear, and so on.

The three vehicles, standard LBS141 and LBS 111 models, were then driven by 112 drivers from 42 different companies to ensure a good statistical spread and test results to provide a realistic picture of the fuel consumption of Swedish rigs under a variety of operating conditions. These test trials continued for 14 months.

This practical approach was only one part of the Scania fuel-economy programme. In a paper delivered at a transport energy conference in June 1978, Scania's assistant managing director, Sverker Sjöström, spoke about how a truck should be used and how equipment should be selected in order to reduce fuel consumption.

In Scania's view, he explained, the most important aspect in order to use fuel in a rational way was selection of truck

Good all-round vision is essential for safe and efficient driving. The three-mirror arrangement fitted here is designed to give not only a total rear view, but also sight of the ground immediately alongside the cab.

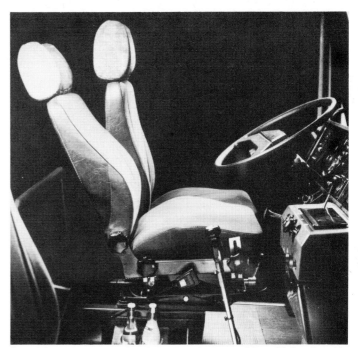

One of Scania's long-held beliefs has been in the provision of fully adjustable backrest, height and springing of the driver's seat.

size and choice of power train combination.

Specific fuel consumption figures could, he said, be used to show how fuel consumption characteristics has been improved over the years. These revealed that Scania's pre-combustion chamber diesel of 1944 had a 35 per cent higher fuel consumption than the DS11 introduced in 1974. Scania's latest high-horsepower, flat-torque engine is, of course, even more fuel efficient than the DS11.

One of the methods Scania had used, Mr Sjöström explained, to improve driving techniques so that the driver used the vehicle in a proper way so as to achieve optimum fuel consumption, was to equip the vehicle with a colour-marked revolution counter so that he knew the most efficient road speed band; green was used for the range up to 1,900 rpm, yellow for 1,900 to 2,200 and red above 2,200.

Cooling fans could add to the fuel consumption of the engine, so a thermostatically-controlled fan, which operated only when needed, had become a standard fitment on Scania models. Scania's experience has been that the thermostatically-controlled fan saved about 4 to 6 per cent of fuel, depending on the type of operation.

Another area fully investigated by Scania has been resistance — air resistance, rolling resistance, gradient resistance and inertia. Adopting a low height, streamlined cab and body design features and using aids like cab wind deflectors to minimize air resistance, could bring economies, Scania found. Use of radial tubeless tyres lessened rolling resistance, but only road builders could help with gradient resistance, although fitment of more powerful engines had a beneficial impact on fuel consumption in this context. Careful, steady driving — the kind of driving encouraged by the Scania fuel-saving project with the road transport organizations — was the way to combat the effects of inertia on a vehicle. A saving of as much as 10 per cent could result from adopting steady driving techniques.

As for optimizing engine and final-drive for a given task, Scania's answer was to plot fuel consumption for a certain drive ratio over a particular route, in this case Stockholm — Gothenburg, and chart the results on vehicles of an otherwise identical specification. This showed there was a minimum point in the fuel consumption for that drive ratio. However, the best compromise had to be sought between fuel consumption and drivability. This showed, for example, that the DS11 engine combined with a final-drive ratio of 4.71:1 offered a fuel saving of 3.5 litres per 100 km when decreasing the speed from 80 km/hr to 70 km/hr and 2.5 litres per 100 km when decreasing from 90 to 80 km/hr.

In order to arrive at optimum engine power, final-drive ratios and optimum fuel consumptions, Scania has introduced its own truck operation simulation programme, which is sufficiently flexible to allow for various driving conditions, such as traffic congestion and sharp bends. The eventual aim is to produce exactly the right vehicle for a particular job.

These efforts to improve fuel economy and an ever-more efficient vehicle reflect yet another aspect of Scania's involvement with the operating side of transport. This facet of Scania's character was particularly noticeable in the 1960s when the company seemed to have been heavily involved not only in producing vehicles but in 'systems' transport to suit individual operators' needs.

A main area of involvement was in demountable body systems. These were particularly attractive in Sweden because of the high gross weights permitted, but they meant relatively slow turn-round on conventional vehicles because of the time needed to load and unload. The ability to mount and dismount a body was also useful because Sweden's climate generally stops building and construction work in the winter months. It is therefore useful to be able to dismount a tipper or mixer body easily and replace it with a tank body for distributing heating oil.

Encouragement of this kind of concept gave Scania a close involvement with the operating side of the industry, which was enhanced by similar links with the main operating co-operative which dominates the Swedish haulage industry — ASG and Bilspedition. As these concerns operate large transport terminals in different parts of the country, Scania has always been able to gather first-class operating knowledge of their products because the co-operatives keep detailed records. Scania also has benefitted in similar ways from the fact that these co-operatives have collection and delivery fleets operating into and from the transport centres.

As Scania also points out, transport problems in food manufacture and the grocery trade have been largely solved by the merger of wholesalers into a few large distribution companies, such as ICA, Konsum and DAGAB. These large companies have established major terminals at strategic points from which goods are distributed to individual shops.

As all such goods are handled on 700 x 820 mm or 720 x 840 mm pallets, tailormade distribution vehicles loaded with 26 to 28 pallets, or 6 to 7 ton payload, are the result. Use of tailboard loading equipment is now the norm and has been for some years. This close contact with the industry it serves explains, to a large degree, Scania's success in a very competitive environment and is just one more example of why this Swedish company has earned its place in the forefront of heavy commercial vehicle manufacture.

18